The Humm Handbook

Lifting Your Level of
Emotional Intelligence

Christopher Golis
MA, MBA, SF Fin, FAICD

WP

Published by:
Wilkinson Publishing Pty Ltd
ACN 006 042 173
Level 4, 2 Collins Street
Melbourne, Vic 3000
Ph: 03 9654 5446
www.wilkinsonpublishing.com.au

Copyright © Christopher C. Golis 2007

All rights reserved. No part of this publication may be reproduced, stored in a retrieval system or transmitted in any form by any means without the prior permission of the copyright owner. Enquiries should be made to the publisher.

Every effort has been made to ensure that this book is free from error or omissions. However, the Publisher, the Author, the Editor or their respective employees or agents, shall not accept responsibility for injury, loss or damage occasioned to any person acting or refraining from action as a result of material in this book whether or not such injury, loss or damage is in any way due to any negligent act or omission, breach of duty or default on the part of the Publisher, the Author, the Editor, or their respective employees or agents.

Golis, Christopher.

    The humm handbook : lifting your level of emotional intelligence.

    ISBN 9781921332029 (pbk.).

    1. Personnel management. 2. Emotional intelligence. I. Title.

    658.3

Cover and page design by Powerhouse Design
www.powerhousedesign.com.au

Printed in China.

To my elder daughter Louisa
Who, on becoming a manager, asked me 'what books should I read?'

Acknowledgements

It was Charles Handy who started me on the journey and it was he who organised *The Art of Decision-Making* elective at the London Business School. The course was given by a friend of his, William Letwin, and I still regard it as the best course I ever did. Although the application of the classics to business thinking is not new, his course was particularly illuminating.

Kevin Chandler introduced me to the Humm-Wadsworth technology. While I have looked at many other personality analysis technologies, it was the first to be developed and I still think it is the best for understanding the emotional drives of people.

Any faults of interpretation or facts are mine. Susie Welstead and Anna Wallace, the two 'queens' of English Literature, did a terrific job in editing the manuscript and raising a number of interesting questions about my interpretations of the classics. They continue to have the last word.

Contents

Foreword	**1**
Introduction	**3**
Overview	**7**
The Seven Components	**11**
Introduction	12
The Mover	13
The Doublechecker	19
The Artist	27
The Politician	34
The Engineer	42
The Hustler	48
The Normal	55
The Emotionally Intelligent Manager	**61**
Step 1: Self-Awareness	62
Step 2: Self-Management	67
Step 3: Social Awareness	72
Step 4: Relationship Management	79
Building Teams	96
Management Styles	98
Combinations	107
The Glass Ceiling	119
Leadership	122
The Art of Decision-Making	**127**
Introduction	128
Antigone	130
Julius Caesar	139
Hamlet	155
King Lear	164
Death of a Salesman	177
References	**186**

Foreword

During your life you meet many people and occasionally someone who makes a big difference to the path you take. In my case it was Charles Handy, who was my tutor at the London Business School when I was doing a Masters of Business Administration in the early 1970s. Charles subsequently became a well-known management writer; indeed, *Fortune* magazine described him as the best modern management guru of the 1990s.

In my final year as we were all doing job interviews I had the good fortune to be offered a job by McKinseys in New York. When discussing this opportunity with Charles he said that if he were in my position, he would not take the job. In his opinion the most important talent in business was to be good at one-on-one meetings; because that was when decisions were made. However, while MBA courses were good at teaching business analysis they were very poor in developing people skills. He suggested the best way to gain this expertise was to become a capital goods salesperson. This was what Professor Badaracco has called 'defining moment'; a decision point which shapes a person's career. I subsequently went to Australia and following his advice became a trainee salesman with ICL, a British mainframe computer company.

At ICL I was introduced for the first time to the Humm-Wadsworth personality model, which is the technology used in this book. It is fair to say that the training program was a moment of epiphany. Up until then I had believed that deep down all of us were the same. After the training program I realised how different we all were, particularly in how we react emotionally. Subsequently, I used the model very successfully in selling and management. One result of this career choice was that I wrote *Empathy Selling,* which described how to use the Humm-Wadsworth technology in selling situations. In this book I attempt to describe how the technique is useful for managers.

Charles's advice was not his only gift. He organised what I still remember as the best course that I have ever attended called *The Art of Decision-Making.* Each week we would study a classic, such as Shakespeare's *King Lear,* where we would engage in Socratic debate about what the play could teach us as future managers. I still remember many of the lessons. In so many management books the examples soon tire; the heroes of the business world quickly pass. While some companies still bear their founder's name (such as Ford), few of us know about the personality and history of the founders of these companies. Even the names of recent CEOs are soon forgotten. On the other hand the classics live on, and their lessons and characters are timeless.

The objective of this book is to give managers a practical guide to emotional intelligence. It describes a technology for recognising the underlying emotional drives of a person. It then provides a practical guide for managers in how to employ the technology based on the framework of *Emotional Intelligence.* In the final section, *The Art of Decision-Making,* five classic plays are used to provide a further guide for managers. I hope readers find the technique as pragmatic and entertaining as I have.

Introduction

Understanding human nature is a problem that people have been trying to solve throughout the ages. Almost everyone would like to have an understanding of the disposition of those about them so as to be able to predict their behaviour. This is particularly true for managers. Surveys of experienced business managers continuously rank 'people skills' as the most important competence of the successful manager—way above others such as, for example, being a strategic thinker. Great managers have a strong desire to understand the temperament of their subordinates, peers and superiors.

> "There is a very real need among managers to understand what makes people 'tick' — what makes them behave as they do."

Successful managers are generally perceived by their staff to have a genuine concern for their welfare. On the other hand managers must also be seen by their staff as objective and independent. Within every group of employees there are some who are more difficult to manage than others. Some are more responsive to peer pressure, some need to be left alone, some respond best to authoritarian pressure. There is a very real need among managers to understand what makes people 'tick'—what makes them behave as they do.

One of the main errors that people make in trying to understand others is to judge them by their own tendencies. Everyone agrees that human nature is a very complex process and that one person differs greatly from another. However, in our relations with others we are too ready to judge as if everyone acts like we do.

For example, it is a common mistake of those who are easily discouraged to expect others to be as easily discouraged as them by every difficulty. Those who are more selfish than average protect themselves unnecessarily against the selfishness which they expect to find in others. Those with strong self-control and self-discipline tend to be impatient with others who fail to control themselves as successfully.

Temperament is that aspect of personality which deals with the impulsive, emotional, non-rational aspects of behaviour. When we first meet someone we know their personality depends on a number of factors: their level of ability, their motivation in life, their upbringing, family, whether they have children, the organisation they work for, their job in that organisation and many others. Temperament however governs how a person will apply their abilities and experience in making decisions when they are under emotional stress. And it is when people are under emotional stress that managers need all the skills they can muster.

Daniel Goleman published *Emotional Intelligence* in 1995, and since then the concept has become a fixture in the management lexicon. Goleman argued that it was not cognitive intelligence that guaranteed business success but emotional intelligence. He described emotionally intelligent people as those with four characteristics:

1. They were good at understanding their own emotions (self-awareness),
2. They were good at managing their emotions (self-management),
3. They were empathetic to the emotional drives of other people (social awareness), and
4. They were good at handling other people's emotions (relationship management).

Goleman's definition has become widely accepted. The difficulty is that there is not a widely accepted theory of core emotions. While Goleman argues a most persuasive case for the importance of emotions he admits in Appendix A of *Emotional Intelligence* that he has a major problem. He states that he does not have a theory of emotion with which he is comfortable, most particularly in the area of primary emotions. What he does do is quote the discovery of Paul Ekman at the University of California in San Francisco, that facial expressions for four core emotions (fear, anger, sadness, enjoyment) are recognised by people in cultures around the world. This includes people in cultures as remote as the Fore of New Guinea, who live in an isolated Stone Age in the remote highlands. The argument is that if all people, including preliterate people (presumably untainted by exposure to cinema or television) universally recognise these core emotions then they must exist.

Goleman then goes on to list a hierarchy of emotional intensities. He defines an *emotion* as a feeling and its distinctive thoughts, psychological and biological states, and propensity to act such as when we become angry. He then goes on to define a *mood*, which, while more muted, lasts longer than an emotion, and he compares the emotion anger with a grumpy mood. Beyond moods he then defines *temperament*, as the readiness to evoke a given emotion or mood, such as someone with a choleric temperament. Finally he notes there are the outright *disorders* of emotion which can lead to insanity, such as someone with paranoid schizophrenia.

Level of Emotional Intensity	Population Penetration and Frequency
Emotion	All of the people all of the time
Mood	Most of the people some of the time
Temperament	30% of people most of the time
Disorder	1% of people all of the time

As we shall see in the next chapter we will use a theory of core emotions that works in the reverse direction. The model considers the basic mental disorders and uses them to develop a theory of temperament.

It should be noted that this is a different route from that since pursued by Goldman and other human resource specialists. They have adopted a competency based approach.

A competency is a characteristic that allows you to outperform others in a task. They can be personal qualities or attributes, along with skills and experience. Interviewers now do not want to just hear that you are self-starter with initiative but want demonstrable evidence. For example have you had a successful track record in sales? When you were at university did you run a social club or a sports team? This is called the competency-based interview approach.

The difficulty comes when you try to measure Emotional Intelligence competencies such as empathy. For example I have seen it suggested that empathy be assessed on criteria such as the ability to develop rapport; making and sustaining informal contacts with people in addition to the contacts required for work, having the ability to chat about non-work issues; and participation in a broad range of social relationships. In other words can you prove that you are a people person?

Some people are naturally more empathetic than others but if you are not naturally a people person are there ways you can become more empathetic? How do you put yourself in someone else's shoes? Can you change tack after thinking through someone else's emotional reaction to your first approach? And what is the best tack to take?

One way of developing empathy is to do a job that requires it, such as selling. That is what happened to me. Another way is to ask family and friends about the way you come across. Personal coaching can also be tried but it is relatively expensive.

In this book we adopt a different approach. First we learn a scientific model of people's underlying emotions. We then use this model to dramatically increase your four EQ competencies: self-analysis, self-control, empathy and relationship management. You will learn to become a better manager and leader. Finally we use the model to analyse five cases studies taken from the world of theatre.

Overview

It is safe to say that there is no time in history when people have not tried to make sense out of the behaviour of other people, usually in terms of a relatively simple descriptive model. The Greek physician, Hippocrates (ca. 460-370 B.C.), for example, identified four basic humours, or body fluids, which he thought were related to a variety of conditions, including temperament. Five hundred years later the physician and scientist Galen (130-200 A.D.), who advanced the traditions of Hippocrates, identified these humours with specific temperamental characteristics, as described below:

- The *sanguine* person is characterised by the tendency to be overly cheerful, optimistic, vain, and unpredictable. Such a person is usually in danger of being taken advantage of. In Hippocrates' terms, a sanguine person's physiology was dominated by blood.
- The *phlegmatic* person is nonchalant, unemotional, cool, persevering, and needing direction. The physiology of such an individual was thought to be dominated by phlegm.
- The *melancholic* person, characterised by the dominance of black bile, is slow in responding, soft-hearted, and oriented towards doing things for others.
- Persons of the *choleric* temperament are domineering, stubborn, opinionated, and self-confident. Their physiology is dominated by yellow bile.

These four dispositions have remained in our language for describing persons, although the biological causes of them have, of course, been discarded.

However, it is only in the last century that psychologists have developed techniques to scientifically analyse personality. Psychologists, aided by computers have refined personality questionnaires considerably. Modern psychological profiles have now been produced which are completely descriptive of the person tested. Modern theory now uses between sixteen to twenty components of personality to analyse people's emotional behaviour.

Many people are as yet unawares of the sophistication of personality testing and the discrimination that researchers have managed to build into their tests. I remember a feature article in an English Sunday newspaper in the late 1960s, which described an experiment where a psychologist had seven famous people complete a personality test questionnaire. From the test results the psychologist produced seven psychological profiles which in turn were all sent to the seven participants, who were asked to choose the one they thought best described their own personality.

The results of the experiment were illuminating—each of the seven participants correctly chose his own profile! The odds of this occurring are 1 in 823,543 or slightly more than picking the ace of spades three times in row from a pack of shuffled cards. I remember, on reading this article, being surprised that personality testing had reached such a level of precision.

The problem with modern theory is that sixteen to twenty components is too many for the average person to remember so there have been many attempts to simplify the analysis. In this book we are going use a theory that uses seven components.

In 1924 an American psychologist, Rosanoff, first proposed the model we are going to use. Until the work of Rosanoff, doctors defined abnormal psychological conditions in black and white: people were either mad or not. Rosanoff suggested that such a distinction between the normal and abnormal states was artificial and the difference was not one of *kind* but of *degree*. Normality and abnormality should not be thought of as black and white but as different shades of grey.

Whether there is a sharp division between sanity and insanity is still a matter of debate. The first person to develop a scientific system of classification of mental illness was Emil Kraeplin of Germany. Searching for patterns in hundreds of case studies, Kraeplin proposed two broad categories of mental illness: schizophrenia and manic depression. Kraeplin began a more generalised approach to diagnosing symptoms, which is the basis for today's diagnostic bible in psychiatry, the *Diagnostic and Statistical Manual of Mental Disorders (DSM-IV)*. The classification of mental illnesses has become a growth industry: The first edition of DSM, published in 1952, described just over 60 disorders; the latest, revised in 2000, lists about 400 disorders. It is estimated that the DSM-V due to be published in 2010 will contain about 1800 disorders and generate about $80 million sales for its publishers, the American Psychiatric Association. As the number of known mental illnesses increases; so too the number of specialised drugs that need to be developed by the major pharmaceutical companies.

Increasingly the validity of this approach has been questioned and drug companies have been forced to remove treatment claims. For example, the drug company

Lilly is no longer allowed to claim Prozac treats premenstrual dysphoric disorder because the European drug regulator found *'the condition was not a well-established disease entity.'*

Richard Bentall in his recent book, *Madness Explained: Psychosis and Human Nature in Medicine,* argues that the difference between sanity and insanity is more subtle and less defined. He argues the model should not be bi-polar but more of a continuum, supporting the original concept of Rosanoff.

Rosanoff, using the work of Kraeplin, further noted there were few mental illnesses and proposed a theory of personality based on the most common four:

- schizophrenia
- epilepsy
- hysteria
- cyclodia (what we now would call manic-depression)

and a fifth component called the Normal. This component may best be understood as the desire for order and is associated with behaviour such as social adjustment or integration with society. It is best expressed as the gradual change that occurs to the personality as the human being matures—and then may fade away if the adult enters a second childhood.

Two southern Californians, Humm, a statistician, and Wadsworth, a clinical psychologist, using multi-variate factor analysis extended the Rosanoff hypothesis by sub-dividing both cyclodia and schizophrenia into two new components. Cyclodia was divided into manic-depression and schizophrenia divided into autistic-paranoid. The Humm-Wadsworth model thus has seven personality temperament components. For simplicity we are going to refer to the model as the 'Humm'.

The personality stereotypes used in this book lack the precision of subsequent research, but that is not a reason to refuse to use them. A good analogy is the sailors' use of celestial navigation to establish their location. Celestial navigation is based on the hypothesis that the earth is fixed and the stars and the sun revolve around the earth. Since the time of Copernicus we have known this hypothesis to be false, and it is possible to use the laws of relativity to calculate one's position accurately. However, the calculations are laborious and complex and, without a computer, impractical. By using a sextant and the hypothesis that the sun and the stars revolve around a fixed earth, sailors can quite easily fix their position with a degree of accuracy, sufficient for their purposes.

Another advantage of the Humm is that it uses seven components, which is the limit of the short-term memory of most human beings. We are born with two memories, a short-term memory and a long-term memory. Before information is put into our long-term memory, it must go through our short-term memory, which has a maximum limit of seven items. It is for this reason that telephone numbers in most countries are seven digits long. If you have children you soon realise that as they begin to talk they rapidly learn the days of the week. However the names and order the months of the year takes much longer for children to learn.

The seven components that we are going to discuss cover about 90% of our emotional behaviour. We all have these seven components within ourselves, but it is the variation and mix of these components that are reflected in the personality of the individual. In addition, in every individual several components tend to be dominant over time. The secret of the Humm is to learn how to recognise these dominant components and then tailor your management style accordingly.

Now, if a person had only one excessive, dominant desire their personality would deteriorate into a caricature. Such people, it must be stressed, do not exist in real life. Nevertheless, to explain the techniques of the Humm it is convenient to describe hypothetical stereotypes dominated by one desire.

Associated with each of the seven components is a basic desire. While it would be possible to use the original Humm-Wadsworth terms throughout this book, they are alien to most readers and are associated with mental illness. Consequently we have eliminated the jargon and used terms that convey the dominant desire and correlate each component with a stereotype.

The reader should remember when he uses this methodology that it is a simplification and accuracy is sacrificed.

Stereotype	Dominant Desire	Original Humm-Wadsworth Term
Normal	Desire for order	Normal
Mover	Desire to communicate	Manic
Doublechecker	Desire for security	Depressive
Artist	Desire to be creative	Autistic
Politician	Desire to win	Paranoid
Engineer	Desire to complete projects	Epileptoid
Hustler	Desire for material success	Hysteroid

Now, when describing someone Humm users often just use the first letter of the stereotype. Thus, we may call someone a little 'H' or big 'P', a strong 'E' or a weak 'D', a high 'M' or a low 'N'. Fans of the Humm describe using these abbreviations as 'Humm-talk'. Remember that each of these seven desires is present in all of us and sometime or other each affects our behaviour. For example in an argument the P component comes to the fore, but while decorating a room or going to an art gallery, the A component will tend to dominate.

The Seven Components

Introduction

The following seven chapters discuss each of the personality stereotypes in depth. After an introduction each chapter contains a short dialogue between you and an imaginary employee of the relevant stereotype. The next section then describes the clues that allow you to identify the prospect's dominant component. Then we discuss how a personality totally obsessed by this desire would behave. In reality, and this cannot be stressed enough, few personalities are completely dominated by one desire. However, it is easier to understand each type by describing a theoretical individual dominated by one desire. In this way the reader should develop empathy with each of the seven temperament types. To help in understanding, examples are taken from two classic marketing areas—the dominant themes in different decades as reflected in the films and advertising and the type of car the theoretical individual would most likely buy. After the house, a car is perhaps the next most expensive item most people would buy. Automobiles in particular are as much an emotional purchase as a rational one.

To provide a contrast, the personality of someone lacking the particular desire is briefly described. These opposite personalities are more difficult to detect but it can be useful to identify them when deciding on a management approach.

Most people lack the instinct or intuition of the great writers; they assume that other people act and behave just as they themselves do, with only limited variation. Only when managers develop the skills of self-analysis and empathy do they begin to understand how diverse people really are.

The Mover

In the BBC television series, *Life on Earth*, David Attenborough described humans as 'the compulsive communicators'. He postulated that the human being's passion to give and receive communication was as important to our success as the fin was to the fish or the feather to the birds. This desire to communicate is probably the most basic and common of all desires and that is why the Mover is perhaps the most common dominant desire. In the cameo below we describe the stereotype of a prospect dominated by this one desire.

Movers are often found working in organisations that require a lot of contact with people. Good examples would be the fast food, car rental and retail industries.

In this case the employee's name is Gerry Grasshopper, who is a product manager. In Aesop's fable of the grasshopper and the ant, the former is a typical Mover—the grasshopper flits around, is perennially optimistic, never worries about the future, and thinks with its heart and not with its head.

The individual concerned is an imaginary amalgam of several individuals I have met during my career. The incidents that occurred during this imaginary conversation have all happened.

First meeting with a Mover

Gerry Grasshopper is a marketing manager for Hamburger Hut, a leading chain of fast food outlets. Gerry is working on a new promotion for his company; a toothbrush that bends under the hot water tap to any shape one wants, remaining in its new position once the plastic has cooled. Children thought the toothbrushes were great fun and as kids are the decision-makers for fast food restaurants, Gerry thought it would be a great marketing campaign for

Hamburger Hut. You have been brought in as an external consultant by senior management to review the proposal.

The head office of Hamburger Hut is hidden away off a freeway behind large trees. There were two receptionists at the desk and, between the constant phone calls, I managed to hand across my card and announce my presence. People were everywhere. On the walls were posters of various advertising campaigns and charities with which Hamburger Hut was involved. I joined the six other people waiting in reception.

Twenty minutes after the scheduled time for the appointment, a small man burst through the doors from the head office into the reception area. He was not wearing a coat. His sleeves were rolled up to his elbows and his collar was unbuttoned at the top.

'Hi, Donna. Where's the consultant?'

'Over there in the grey suit and the blond hair.'

He strode across and breathlessly apologised for being late. 'Sorry, we just had an impromptu meeting of the social club. We are organising a horse riding weekend and somebody wanted the company to organise insurance. 'Have a go,' I said, 'let people organise their own insurance if they are worried.' Now, it's Jim, isn't it?'

'Yes, Mr Grasshopper,' I said, extending my hand into his back.

Mr Grasshopper had spun around and now was talking to someone else.

'Bill, isn't it? Didn't we meet about three months ago at the Big Potato Golf Day?'

'Yes, Gerry, it was a great day wasn't it?'

'Terrific, met some great people. Say, why, don't you pop down to my office when you are through and have a cup of coffee. I would love to talk with you—you wouldn't mind, would you Jim?' he said turning back to me and giving me another big smile.

'No trouble at all, Mr Grasshopper.'

'Call me Gerry, Jim, everyone does.'

'Yes, Gerry,' I said, meanwhile thinking to myself that it really helps a consultant interview to have a complete stranger interrupt it in the middle for a cup of coffee.

We started to move across the reception area to the head office entrance when suddenly Gerry dashed back to the reception area.

'Any messages?'

'Yes, Gerry. We have two that have just come in. The advertising agency wants you to see the video of the new advert and a cable TV station wants to talk to you about a new programme that targets the children's market.'

'Right, well,' he looked at me then at his watch. 'Email them and tell them I will ring them later.'

He turned round, gave me an emphatic come-on signal with his right hand and said, 'Well, it's 11:30. Let's get going.'

We burst through the door and sprinted down the hall to his office. On the way Gerry said hello to seven people, three pot plants and one closing door.

We finally got to his office. Advertising boards were everywhere. A long, low filing cabinet had papers scattered across the top and his desk was filled with more files, knickknacks, executive toys, and telephone messages.

The phone rang. Gerry picked it up instantly.

'Gerry here. Hi Fred. How's the wife and kids. No. Yes. No. Look I'll ring you later. I have someone with me at the moment.'

Gerry then dialled his receptionist on the hands-free phone. 'Roxie, will you take a drinks order please?'

'Get me a diet Coke. What will you have Jim?'

'Oh, a natural spring water would be nice.'

'And hold the calls Roxie,' said Gerry and he pressed the disconnect button.

'I hate doing that but the boss says you have to focus on the job at hand.'

Gerry smiled at me and I smiled back.

'Right now let's talk about the greatest marketing idea I have ever seen—the bendable toothbrush.'

Profile of a Mover

It is easy to recognise people with reasonably strong Mover characteristics—they are always smiling. They are cheerful, outgoing, warm and enthusiastic. Because they are dominated by the desire to communicate they project optimism and relish social activity. They are the individuals who get up at 5:30 am to go jogging with a group of friends. Movers will share in a car pool to commute to the office. After a workday full of meetings, the Mover then loves to take part in some active social entertainment in the evening such as a party or going dancing.

Every so often there is a pause in this frenetic activity. An outburst of emotion will suddenly occur accompanied with statements such as 'It's impossible—I can't go on.

Nobody listens or cares after all I do for them.' This short piece of melodrama is soon over and forgotten, the batteries are recharged and the whirl of social activity restarts.

People with an excess of the Mover component (or big Ms as they are more affectionately known) are good-natured, and easily approachable, though they can become impatient at times. Ms are optimistic and enthusiastic about life, easily excitable, talkative and laugh readily. Movers tell jokes about other people and joke about themselves. They are the ones who when they get a joke email send it to 30 other people immediately. Movers are ready to co-operate and like to participate in social activities. They have strong, emotional likes and dislikes, and their one big dislike is people who they feel are 'cold fish'.

> "...the easiest way to first recognise Movers is by their friendly and enthusiastic smile."

Movers are distractible, their attention is easily diverted and they dislike detail. Ms like to look at the big picture; otherwise they can become easily bored.

Probably the easiest way to first recognise Movers is by their friendly and enthusiastic smile. Movers will soon be on first name terms with you. When you meet them they will often be wearing bright, colourful clothing. Ms like clothes that are trendy, fun, and they enjoy going to fancy-dress parties. Jeans, sports shoes, a bright sweater or shirt typifies the Mover. In the office environment they generally work with their coats off, their sleeves rolled up, and quite often their hair is messy and their neck tie will be undone. The women prefer shorter hair, as it is easier to maintain and wear simple natural makeup, and often wear big jangling bracelets and earrings.

The 1920s was a Mover decade—the boom mentality, perennial optimism and the social whirl all typify the Mover. The frenetic activity of the Charleston, the popularity of clubs and nightspots and the mergers in the business community in that era all indicate the dominance of the Mover component.

The cars they drive depend on whether they're married or not. If single, they like fast, bright, sporty cars, ones that can zip around the place and take them from social gathering to social gathering. Once they are married and have children, Movers then look for people movers. They still like them to have a bit of zip and speed but they're into station wagons or SUVs, because then they're ferrying children from place to place. However, in both cases the cars are often messy.

Indeed, Movers are not the tidiest people in the world. If you go into their bedroom it is often strewn with clothes and if you go into their offices the desks are often untidy as they drop one activity and move on to the next. It's not that they don't care, rather that Movers start tasks enthusiastically yet often lack the concentration to finish, so their desks are usually cluttered. Movers are often distracted by the telephone. When it rings, they instantly pick it up and start talking—they love distractions, especially if it means further social contact

They're often late for meetings and appointments because they have been distracted by a previous activity; they rush in breathlessly and then say, 'I'm awfully sorry, but...' Their optimistic enthusiasm soon makes everyone forgive them for their tardiness.

When you first meet Movers, they will quickly shake hands with you, putting their hands out first, give you a warm smile, and immediately start calling you by your first name. They will socialise before coming to business, telling you of some personal incident of the previous night or earlier in the day. Their voices are quick and enthusiastic. Movers appear sanguine, buoyant and fidgety. The flow of the Mover's conversation is changeable and will often suddenly switch direction. Movers frequently use vigorous gestures while they talk.

They tend to see issues in black and white and prefer action to thought. People sometimes criticise Movers for being impulsive and showing poor attention to detail, but if their decisions are successful, people forget the criticism and praise the Mover for rapid analysis and audacity.

Because they have sunny dispositions yellow is the Mover colour. It is no coincidence that the largest fast food chain in the world, McDonalds, and the largest car rental company, Hertz, both have yellow as their dominant colour.

People with low Mover component appear to be cold, colourless and phlegmatic. Low Movers appear dull and drab and are at a distinct disadvantage in western society with its norms based on social activity and contact.

On the other hand, people with a strong Mover component can sometimes be trying as individuals. They like, and want, to interact socially and need to receive affection in return. Some people consider they overreact and are too mercurial. Movers can be insensitive, too, in the way they force their optimism onto everyone else; their feverish imploring to 'cheer up and smile' can sometimes become tiresome.

Movers, because they need excitement and change, tend to switch jobs and friends easily—for them loyalty is a temporary feeling. As Movers may be mercurial both in personality and friendships, people sometimes suspect them of insincerity. This is unjust, however; the Mover will not deceive deliberately. Unfortunately Movers are so impulsive they sometimes do things that unwittingly hurt and offend more sensitive people.

At work Movers may be disruptive, since they lack self-control. Their desire to communicate means that they may distract their fellow workers with conversation and chatter. They have a tendency to start a task with enthusiasm but their interest soon expires; they start evening courses, for example, and then leave after several weeks. Their backyards are full of half finished boats. If you give them a deadline they usually fail to meet it. On the other hand, if you give them a job that requires meeting lots of people and having little responsibility or concern for the long-term, they are excellent performers.

Successful business people often have a high Mover component as this provides them with the necessary energy, drive and enthusiasm to succeed. Successful people in sales, public relations or personnel usually have a large amount of Mover component. Ms also like working in service areas such as retailing, fast food, or car rental. The worst jobs for Movers are ones that coop them up in an office alone without a phone.

Every component has strengths and weaknesses. People with the high Mover component, will build up enthusiasm for new programs and their sociability means that they can work well in groups. On the other hand, having a lot of Mover does have some weaknesses. Movers do not finish what they start. They sometimes disrupt the work of others by their jolly, talkative, and emotional behaviour. Also, they may do a job in a superficial way, and in work that requires repetition and methodical attention to detail they may end up becoming irresponsible and unreliable.

The Doublechecker

After the desire to communicate, the next most common desire is probably for security. The Doublechecker is the stereotype in whom this desire is dominant. We all have some need for security in our personalities but for some this desire is stronger than others. These people are probably first recognised by their strong sense of obligation. They're very sensitive to other peoples' approval and disapproval. They are easily touched and often show compassion to others. If energised by this concern they can put a lot effort into getting something done such as installing a new personnel system or collecting for a charity.

They often, for no apparent reason, have feelings of insecurity and inadequacy. Doublecheckers are a bit like rabbits, they're over-anxious and worrisome. If something new comes along, they either retreat back into the burrow, or are pessimistic about its chances of success. They're hesitant and indecisive about decisions, which is why they are called Doublecheckers. They need encouragement and reassurance. Doublecheckers find it hard to get started on something. But when they finally do start, they will go through and complete it with an energy that quite surprises their colleagues.

In the following meeting I have used as an employee, Rachel Rabbit, who is a payroll administrator. For both the preparation and maintenance of payroll information most organisations would prefer to employ somebody who has security uppermost in mind and who is also a compulsive double checker of computer input and output. Most employees and organisations want to keep payroll and personnel information confidential; most managers also know that mistakes in a payroll can be a major cause of disharmony in an organisation.

First meeting with a Doublechecker

Rachel Rabbit was the senior pay mistress for a large factory that had been built fifty years ago. I had recently been appointed Group Financial Controller and this was our first meeting.

I arrived five minutes early and was immediately directed to the pay office. On arrival I was shown in. The office had wall-to-wall filing cabinets and stacked on each cabinet was a metre-high pile of bound computer printouts. The desk was heaped with files. On the desk was a packet of cigarettes and a lighter. By the telephone was a photograph of three children, a man and Ms Rabbit, which I guessed had been taken about three years ago.

Ms Rabbit was wearing a brown cardigan over a beige dress. She had on little make up, was wearing an expensive watch and a pair of very expensive glasses. I handed across my card. Her handshake was weak.

> 'What a coincidence; my youngest son is named Jim. My name is Rachel.'

> 'Good afternoon, Rachel. How's the day been?'

> 'Oh, the usual disasters. The computer's down, the courier's late, I still have a terrible cough and the general manager wants a special labour costing report by tonight.'

> 'Not feeling well then?'

> 'No, there is a pain between my shoulders under my neck. These glasses are giving me a headache and my knee is playing up. Gosh, I just remembered.'

> She poured out a glass of water. 'It's time for my pills.' From her desk drawer she took out three bottles.

> 'What are they all for?'

> 'The white ones are calcium, the brown ones garlic and the green capsules supercharged B vitamins.'

> 'Well they should help you feel well. How's the family?'

> 'Oh I don't know. My youngest son just won't study and the eldest now wants to get married. I am worried about his girlfriend. She looks flighty to me, I'm sure it won't last.'

> 'Yes, well, it's a big decision and ...'

> Just then the phone rang. I waited.

> 'No ... you can't be serious ... this place is never going to survive another six months ... I knew the old financial controller was given the push and the voluntary retirement was just a cover ... Oh I don't know ... we will just have

to stick it out ... How's your neck? My sinus is still playing up; it must be the pollen in the air ... Look I better hang up. I have someone with me. See you in 45 minutes for a cigarette break outside.'

'Good friend?'

'That was Madge in creditors. She has just been told to pay no cheques for the next two weeks without the boss's signature. I tell you this company is going to be bankrupt by Christmas. Just my luck—the only fun I ever have is at the office party.'

'Well, I'm sure it can't be as bad as you think. Now I understand you are having problems with your current payroll systems supplier?'

'Problems? I knew I was too rash when I chose them over five years ago. It has been a catastrophe. The support staff are unprofessional. They are too slow to respond to customer requests and the software is riddled with bugs.'

'Riddled?'

'Yes, remember four years ago when they changed the tax scales.'

'Yes, I vaguely remember.'

'Well they had made a mistake in one of the cut-off points. It was $34,999 instead of $35,000 which meant employees would pay 1 cent more tax a week. Well, I was on the phone to them at least five times a day. It took them three days before it was fixed. All they could offer was the lame excuse that the government had made a typographical error in the schedules. They should have checked the original proclamation; it was there in black and white.'

'Any other problems?'

'Well, the staff, they are always changing. I get one payroll analyst then three months later she rings up and tells me she is being promoted or transferred and then I have to get to know a new one.'

'You meet regularly?'

'Every week. I like to have a visit each week where we review the running of the previous week. We spend about an hour on it.'

'Oh,' I thought to myself, that this is a good use of staff resources. 'Anything you dislike about the present reports?' I said bracing myself.

'Well where should we begin?' said Rachel lighting another cigarette.

Profile of a Doublechecker

The timid, nervous, indecisive civil servant best personifies the Doublechecker. Many women have an influential Doublechecker component. The primary drive of the Doublechecker is the desire for security. All through the day the Doublechecker imagines events that can go wrong. At night they dream of disasters.

> "Doublecheckers are customarily dissatisfied and like to complain."

When you first meet Doublecheckers (or big Ds) you can recognise them by their dress and appearance. It is usually conservative and practical. The haircuts of the men tend to be short back and sides and the women, too, have conservative hairstyles. The men often wear brown or grey sweaters and the women typically wear beige. Their dress is earth colours. In terms of their watches and jewellery, they're practical and like quality. The men often wear brown ties or ties with crests representing membership of a large institution. The women carry large handbags full of make-up and accessories to cater for every possible occasion. They often carry a scarf or umbrella because it might rain.

Doublecheckers don't like dangerous activities—they don't do bungee jumping. They play sports that are social but non-dangerous such as tennis and golf. Doublecheckers also tend to look at activities that lead to self-improvement, for they feel that they should be better than they are, consequently these are people who go and do home study and night courses.

Doublecheckers are frequently dissatisfied with their lot in life and often complain or criticise. Ds are often hypochondriacs; ask them how they feel today and in a few minutes you begin to wonder how they are still alive.

The list of their illnesses often includes the following (at least):

- funny spasms in the neck
- unusual fatigue
- aching legs
- indigestion and a funny stomach
- migraine
- spots in the eyes
- fallen arches
- palpitating heart.

When reciting the above list, Doublecheckers frequently intersperse the items with deep sighs. Ds are often smokers. While they may have started smoking to gain social approval, Ds in particular find it difficult to change habits, particularly an addictive one like smoking.

Female Doublecheckers are always snagging nails, having runny eyes or trouble with their hair. Ds have their teeth capped and are always changing glasses or contact lenses because the present ones are unsatisfactory. The outside observer, because these troubles are invisible, sometimes suspects them to be imaginary or trifling.

Ds fill the desk in their offices and the medicine chest in their homes with medicines to counter all types of imaginary ailments. Many of these nostrums should be thrown away, because most have long since lost any effectiveness, but Doublecheckers cannot bear to throw anything away in case it might be useful later. They are magpies and typically hoard everything, as they never know when it might come in handy. Hence their houses generally collect cupboards and chests while the office gathers filing cabinets. Ds will often make a paper copy of everything including simple emails. Their in-trays rapidly fill with correspondence. Ds usually have at least one picture of the family in the office and their homes contain many pictures of the family. This is because Doublecheckers associate the family with security.

Doublecheckers are customarily dissatisfied and like to complain. If something is not wrong with them then there is something wrong with work, friends or the house. Their blood type is definitely B-negative. The only time they cheer up is when they come across someone in a miserable state and is really suffering. The Doublechecker then shows an enthusiastic compassion that may even appear morbid—they will listen to every detail of the trouble, expressing sympathy at every opportunity, continually asking if the poor sufferer has told him everything. This capacity to listen to other people's misfortunes makes them good friends and in the office they often fulfil the role of a parent figure. The old saying *Misery loves company* was coined with the Doublechecker in mind.

When something eventually does go wrong then the Doublechecker tends to exaggerate the disappointment. Even if the matter is trifling, such as a standard seasonal decline in profits or late delivery of stock, the Doublechecker will exaggerate the incident, typically as proof that the firm is on the verge of bankruptcy and will never be able to recover its tattered reputation. Even if the matter does not affect the present, the future effects will be calamitous. The Doublechecker is always thinking about the future and how next year will be terrible. In fact, they so often project gloom that colleagues will sometimes refuse to work with them, citing reasons such as poor attitude and continual complaints.

> "Their blood type is definitely B-negative."

Because Doublecheckers are so influenced by the desire for security and so dread possible calamities, they hesitate about making decisions for fear of the outcome. They tend to favour the status quo especially if it needs little activity, and so they tend to appear mentally vague and physically inactive; they prefer to stay in bed as it is comfortable. Their innate anxiety and indecisiveness can make them seem passive and dull—when you have a conversation with a Doublechecker the initial impression is often one of uncertain passivity.

Doublecheckers procrastinate over the smallest decision, going through both sides of the argument thoroughly. They will ask everyone for opinions, then equivocate and so disregard all the advice. This hesitancy, of course, frequently infuriates the givers of advice. They will also double-check every item of a proposal, use an outside expert to ensure accuracy and then ask for another draft in a different coloured binder. Doublechecker employees tend to exasperate their superiors as they often ask for unnecessary approvals and sanctions.

As a general rule, Doublecheckers make excellent public servants. Ds often work in clerical and administrative positions. Their habit of double-checking everything makes them excellent employees in areas where accuracy is a requirement. Thus stuffed filing cabinets and filled in-trays decorate administration offices around the world. The employees of Doublechecker managers become frustrated as nothing new ever seems to get done and every decision is so exhaustively reviewed that the cost of making the decision begins to outweigh the potential benefits. Government departments sometimes spend hundreds of thousands of dollars evaluating proposals that will only cost thousands to implement.

The 1930s, the time of the Great Depression, is the era dominated by the Doublechecker mentality. The early part of the decade was characterised by governments failing to take decisions. Innovation in many areas stopped. The advertising and films of the era were filled with cigarettes and stressed security and quality. When Ds finally make a decision they tend to choose goods that are of the highest quality and good reputation. They justify this approach by reasoning that cheaper goods will deteriorate more quickly and that you can never go wrong if you choose good quality.

Doublecheckers drive cars that are safe and reliable such as a white or yellow Volvo. If they cannot afford a Volvo they will purchase a brown or pale green Toyota.

The strengths of a Doublechecker are several. Firstly, they're dissatisfied with things as they are. This is a motivation for self-improvement. If you ask the Doublechecker to criticise something they can generally give you a number of reasons. Ds are very careful and methodical in their work. They carefully consider a proposition before taking action. Indeed, they double-check everything.

Doublecheckers are not impetuous or impulsive like the Movers. They also expect things to be a little unpleasant at times, they don't expect too much. Doublecheckers make good deputy managers. They are very good at following a leader, sweeping up the debris of decision making, and making sure everything is bedded down so that it will operate smoothly. If they believe in a project they can attack it with surprising energy. Doublecheckers are notoriously slow starters and some people think their inert passivity is laziness. They will complain in the morning about doing the same task every day and usually need some encouragement to get going. Yet once Ds get into the swing of the task at hand, especially if it is familiar, they cheer up. The Doublechecker is genuinely surprised to find that, at the end of the day, people still remember their bad humour and uncertainty of the early morning.

As with other components the Doublechecker also has weaknesses. They can be quite worrisome. In fact, they so worry about a number of minor issues that it causes other people to become dissatisfied with them. They complain about the lack of opportunities when they may be surrounded by them. Often their desire for security will cause them to pass up good opportunities. Ds make little progress on their own. As mentioned earlier, Doublecheckers are really happy with the status quo; they criticise and complain about it but when you suggest they make a change they say, no, no, no, that's too difficult or that's too hard. Too little

Doublechecker component in a personality leads to impulsive, reckless behaviour. Low Doublecheckers have little compassion for the suffering of others and have no misgivings about their actions. They tend to make decisions impulsively and will often buy from the first salesperson they see.

As stated before, every individual has some degree of each of the seven temperament components in their personality. A later section will cover combinations but the Mover-Doublechecker combination is a common type of personality. People with a strong Mover or Doublechecker usually appear to have a reasonable degree of the other component because they share the same base personality factor—high emotionality. These people often describe themselves as being either up or down. As the name suggests, the two components tend to dominate behaviour alternately. At the extreme, a Mover-Doublechecker can exhibit the moody, mercurial behaviour of the manic-depressive. The amount of time that either component controls the personality depends on its relative strength. However, at various times the other component will govern behaviour.

The Artist

Scientific testing has postulated the presence of over twenty different personality factors. The first factor usually extracted in personality testing is the degree of emotion often shown by a person. Emotionality underlies two connected temperament types, the Mover and the Doublechecker. Both these types centre on feelings and emotions and how a person relates to his environment. Individuals who have a high degree of these two types in their personality react strongly to outside stimuli and are strongly influenced by their senses. They project energy outwards, in the form of optimism, in the case of the Mover, or pessimism in the case of the Doublechecker. The Mover and the Doublechecker are both extrovert temperament components. It is time to discuss the introvert components—the Artist, the Politician, and the Engineer.

> "The creative desire is one of the most basic in mankind and if it is dominant it leads to the Artist stereotype."

As we shall see later most adults tend to have one influential extrovert component and one influential introvert component, along with average-to-strong Normal. If, on the other hand, the two dominant components are both introvert ones, then the person will tend to exhibit the introvert behaviour first characterised by Jung.

Introverts, as a rule, tend to be inward looking people who care more for their own company than that of others. The Artist, Politician and Engineer all have the capacity to handle mental, abstract concepts, but besides having different dominant desires the three temperaments differ in the kinds of information they prefer to process and in how they think. In general, Artists are visual, Politicians are aural and Engineers are tactile.

Twenty thousand years before people began to farm or lived in cities, they had started to paint. In caves in Southern France and in Spain archaeologists have discovered cave paintings of superb quality. The creative desire is one of the most basic in mankind and if it is dominant it leads to the Artist stereotype. In the following discussion the Artist is an architect and, again, a fusion of several people I have known. I have called him Mr Clarence Clam as Artists are generally so tight-lipped they can be particularly awkward customers.

First meeting with an Artist

I was on my way to see Clam & Coral, a leading architectural practice in the city that had an outstanding reputation. Our company needed to appoint a firm of architects for a new office block and I had been given the mandate to develop a shortlist of suitable candidates. My appointment was with Mr Clarence Clam who was the Managing Partner. Most of the city architects were keen to be on the shortlist but it had been difficult to get an appointment with Mr Clam.

The offices of Clam and Coral were located in a restored warehouse in an old quarter of the city. The office reception area was unusual as the walls had been stripped back to the original sandstone. The ceiling had also been removed and the old beams and rafters were visible. Hanging on the wall were drawings and photographs of buildings and some exceptionally colourful works of modern art. There was also what looked like a painted refrigerator.

The receptionist was wearing a dress with an unusual blend of colours and patterns and a pair of very exotic earrings. At exactly ten o'clock the receptionist was buzzed and she led me to the office of Mr Clam. Mr Clam's office was set in the corner of the building which caught the morning sun. As I walked in the first item I noticed was a singular piece of modern sculpture in one corner. In another corner Mr Clam had put a large drawing easel. The office, because it was located in the corner of the building, had two large windows in adjoining walls. Mr Clam had positioned his desk in the corner which faced away from the spectacular views.

I approached his desk and, since he was still reading, coughed gently.

> 'Mr Clam, Jim Smith,' I said handing across my card.
>
> He looked at it for a few seconds, stood up and replied, as he slowly extended his hand, 'Yes, Mr Smith. How can I help you?'
>
> His grip was loose and the handshake was short. We both sat down, he doing so rather quickly. As I slowly seated myself I noticed he was wearing a very modern French leather jacket over an expensive, open-necked, silk shirt. Underneath his thick beard he had tied a fashionable silk scarf around his neck.

'Good view.'

'Many people think so. Personally I find it rather distracting.' His voice was quiet, almost timid.

'Oh. Do you know anyone at Build & Better?'

'Yes. I have met M----,' he mumbled, with his hand over his mouth.

'Sorry. I didn't catch the name.'

'Mr Melrose.'

'Ah yes, Mike Melrose. Great guy. Good tennis player. Have you ever played tennis with him?'

'No. I don't tend to socialise with other architects. Too many are show-offs or have tunnel vision.'

'Oh, but you know his work?'

'Yes.'

'The Winchester Town Hall was one of his. What did you think of that?'

'Good.'

'Good?'

There was a long pause. I had so far not made eye contact with Mr Clam. I then noticed that I was leaning forward in my chair. I sat back rather noisily, crossed my legs, put my elbows on the arms of the chair, and joined my hands in an extended prayer position in front of my face.

Mr Clam looked me in the face for the first time and said, in a slightly relaxed voice, 'I thought the use of perspective in the atrium very imaginative.'

'Anything else?'

'Beyond a shadow of a doubt it is an outstanding building.'

I said to myself that this is going to take some time.

Profile of an Artist

The Artist is dominated by the desire to create. Genesis was a solitary affair and from that time onwards creation has usually been a lonely activity. Artists (also referred to as As) often appear as quiet, shy withdrawn people. They are easy to recognise because they avoid eye contact, the males often have beards and they are initially tongue-tied. As they talk, Artists tend to put their hands over their mouths or faces. They appear to wish to avoid socialising or contact with the environment. If an Artist has an office with a spectacular view the desk is sometimes positioned so the view cannot be seen—As prefer the creative imagination to reality.

> "As Artists generally have good visual imaginations their dress sense is creative and colourful. Sometimes however they go to the opposite extreme and dress themselves 100% in black"

Artists think in pictures and so tend to use visual words such as 'clear', 'show', 'appears' and 'look'. They also use visual expressions such as:

'I get the picture.'

'I see what you mean.'

'That's a sight for sore eyes.'

'I take dim view of that.'

'In the light of ...'

'Let's put things into perspective.'

As Artists generally have good visual imaginations their dress sense is creative and colourful. Sometimes however they go to the opposite extreme and dress themselves 100% in black. Nevertheless, As will tend to be the first to adopt new, imaginative fashions. The clothing and dress of the Artist is generally imaginative, even slightly oddball. Artists generally choose clothes that are high quality and often artistic. On the other hand, because they can become very aloof, they sometimes may disregard their appearance totally. A classic example was Vincent Van Gogh who when he mutilated his ear, demonstrated how individualistic and disregarding of society Artists can be. In terms of accessories such as watches and jewellery, they wear very good, unusual designs or none at all. Artist men, if they wear ties, tend to wear those that are floral and creative.

Their offices, while neat and tidy are typically aesthetic and full of strong, vivid colours. Artists make good interior designers, architects and, of course, painters.

The first conversation with an Artist is often strained. They do not mix easily and tend not to use first names till they have met you several times. They will not talk about themselves or their families and, if they have self-control, they seem cold and aloof. People sometimes think Artists are snooty but the opposite is true. Artists are easily embarrassed and often have feelings of such social inferiority that they prefer to avoid social contact. They are asocial rather than anti-social and usually have few but very close friends. They have been likened to clams, but clams seem to lead dull and boring lives while Artists, because of their lively and colourful imaginations, have a pleasant time day-dreaming and meditating in flights of fancy. If this behaviour becomes too dominant the individual may withdraw completely from society and go into a catatonic state.

Meditation, beards, imaginative clothes, inarticulate mumbling, and socially indifferent behaviour were the characteristics of the Woodstock generation of the 1960s, so the most successful sales techniques with Artists are those that emulate the advertising of that period. Appeals to being part of a group and how to improve your status are 'out'; appeals to the imaginative, internal self are 'in'. The most successful advertising slogan of all time—'We're number two but we try harder'—was created in the 1960s and is a classic appeal to an Artist. Few firms would publicly admit that they are number two or suggest to the prospect that part of the buying process is to imagine which car rental firm would try harder.

As like unusual cars such as Citroëns or Saabs. These are cars which are renowned for their simple, innovative design and have become classics in their time. Artists are sensitive to all the colours. Of the colours of the spectrum violet, or more particularly the delicate mauve, is one of the most unusual or at least, dramatic.

It is a colour that Artists often use to telling effect. Indeed a purple Saab Coupé (four door sedans are too inviting to crowds) would be the perfect car for the Artist.

People sometimes mistake the quiet of the Artist for timidity. Because the Artist hates to argue, especially in a group, managers often believe that they have won an argument only to later discover the opposite. Artists can be stubborn and once they have made up their minds they are almost impossible to change. They can become dogged in their attitudes and almost rocklike in their silent refusal to accept a change of view. If their feelings are hurt Artists can carry the desire for revenge for a long time and, even if the offence was unintentional or imaginary, still be recalcitrant.

Artists generally have restricted interests. They tend to concentrate on three or four activities and focus their creative imagination on those. They have some difficulty in expressing themselves orally, although they often can write well. When they talk they generally are neither very persuasive nor forceful. Because they are quiet, however, you must not think that they are unhappy; Artists, as we established, have very good imaginations and they spend a lot of their time thinking creatively about different situations in which they are involved. As are do not make the same connection between various things that most of us do. In moving from the detail to the general, they do it differently which is a driver for their creativity.

Artists, because of their visual orientation and creative desire, like to go to films, art galleries and museums. Their hobbies and social activities are the creative ones; music, art or other activities in which they can go out and be with nature, such as bush walking. They sometimes have posters of these on the wall or programmes on their desks or coffee tables. Another clue is fresh flowers, which are often in a distinctive vase. Artists are happy if they are on their own. They don't like playing team sports particularly where they can make a mistake and then be shown up by the rest of the group.

People usually consider individuals with a low Artist component as hard, cold and insensitive. They are usually blunt, direct people who appear to lack finesse. Because they are unaware of social niceties and indifferent to social disapproval, they make good salespeople to large organisations in competitive businesses. Low Artists will usually lack creativity and the ability to visualise new ideas.

Therefore, Artists prefer to work in occupations where they can use their creative talents. They work in architects' offices, textile design, or the creative part of an advertising agency. The Artist, because of his sensitivity and imagination, is able to empathise well with other individuals. They tend to be thoughtful and sensitive and will avoid hurting people. Artists will avoid social embarrassment, however, so they work best in solitary positions. With high intelligence they often make good general managers if few decisions have to be made and conflicts are rare. Avoidance of conflict is another goal of the Artist.

Artists have a number of strengths. They are creative and strive for perfection. This is why they are good people to use in areas such as product design. They are also able to work independently. If you give an Artist a task, you can leave them alone. You will generally find that when he or she returns the job has been done well. They are also considerate, tactful and polite.

Artists, on the other hand, do have some weaknesses. They can have difficulty in making social contacts and, as we know, expressing themselves orally. They may not work well with other people. If they come to a task with fixed ideas that are against the major consensus of a group, they may fiercely protect their own concept with an unbelievable stubbornness. This will typically surprise the other members of the group, who always thought the Artist was a quiet individual who wouldn't say 'boo' to a goose. Another problem with As is that if they are put in positions of authority such as management, they do not discipline well. If there are subordinates who are not performing, because they are sensitive people themselves, they find it difficult to be firm and tell subordinates that they are doing something wrong. Artists avoid confrontation. These are the managers who cannot bear to fire other people because they can so easily imagine what the other person is going through and they think what a trauma it would be if they were dismissed themselves.

The Politician

The desire to win is so widespread among human beings that it is often called the 'competitive instinct'. Whether the desire to win is instinctive or learned is a matter of debate, but the amount of human resources that are devoted to sport all over the world (from children's school sport to the Olympics) is testimony to the desire to win. We all have some of this desire in us, to a smaller or larger degree. I have named the stereotype of a person dominated by a desire to win as the Politician. Politicians (also known as Ps) should not be confused with those individuals who are shrewd and manipulative, namely Hustlers (who we will discuss later).

Politicians are different. They do not resemble foxes; they are lions. They are aggressive, argumentative and stubborn. They can be critical and suspicious of other people and when protecting their beliefs, fiercely dogmatic. Ps hate others criticising their own ideas. If someone who is a subordinate makes a mistake and they are being managed by a Politician, woe betide them, because Politicians demand that people accept responsibility over errors.

First meeting with a Politician

I had now been waiting in the foyer of the head office building of the State Electricity Commission for over thirty minutes. Not that it was an uncomfortable wait. The State Electricity Commission building, like that of many public utilities, was one of the largest and most imposing buildings in the city. The foyer, complete with wall fountains and tapestries, tall indoor palms, and thick Italian leather lounges, was perhaps the most opulent in the city.

I was a partner in a consulting company that specialised in training and organisational development. I had an appointment to see Ms Teresa Lion, the head of personnel, at 10 am. It was now 10.25 and still no one had appeared.

Suddenly I was beckoned across by a receptionist. Waiting for me was a young neatly dressed girl who was introduced as Ms Lion's secretary. The secretary said that Ms Lion would see me now and asked me to accompany her to the lift. We went up to the top floor, through the equally imposing head office foyer, through a security door, then down a set of large circular marble steps which had been built to join the two top floors. We walked to a corner office and I was asked to sit down and wait.

Five minutes later a woman in her mid-thirties appeared.

'Ms Lion?'

'No, no. I am Ms Lion's personal assistant. Follow me please.'

She took me through the secretary's office and into her office which was about twice the size. She went up to a door, knocked twice and waited. About thirty seconds later there was an authoritative 'Enter' and she went inside. She came out about five minutes later.

'Ms Lion will see you now.'

I strode purposefully into the office and nearly tripped as my feet sank into several centimetres of thick pile. Ms Lion was seated at the far end of the room at one of the largest desks I had ever seen. The personal assistant led me across the office. While we trekked across, I could not help noticing a number of degrees, awards and plaques on the walls. Underneath one plaque was a photo of her with the previous Premier of the State.

As we walked up to the desk Ms Lion remained sitting. The PA handed across my card.

'Mr Smith, may I introduce Ms Lion.'

'Everyone calls me Jim,' I said as I held out my hand.

'Everyone, except for a few close important friends, calls me Ms Lion,' she said as she stood up and shook my hand with a firm, dry handshake.

'Sit down, Mr Smith,' she said as she handed across her card.

'Susan, would you please hold all calls, I am not to be disturbed unless it is particularly urgent.'

While this command was being given I looked at her card. Ms Lion was the proud holder of three degrees and a Fellow of two organisations. She was dressed in a simple, classical charcoal grey suit and a simple grey blouse. She was in her mid-forties and was wearing simple earrings and expensive German steel-framed glasses.

'I've heard you belong to the Association of Training Officers', I said.

'I was the President three years ago.'

'Oh, I didn't realise. We moved here from the East Coast two years ago.'

> **"You can quickly recognise the self-importance of Politicians; they generally keep you waiting for an appointment."**

'In addition, I was the recipient in the following year of the inaugural prize for the individual who had done the most to promote industrial training in the state during the previous twelve months. On the wall is a photograph of me accepting the prize from the former State Premier, who is a charming man.'

I turned around and looked at the photograph.

'The idea for the prize was devised by me while I was president of the Association and awarded to me the following year. It also carries with it life membership of the Association.'

'Congratulations.'

'Thank you. Well, Mr Smith, what is your position in the company that you represent? Are you the managing partner?'

'No—we don't have one. We operate as a true partnership. We have a managing committee and the chairperson rotates monthly. I was made a partner when I left my professorship five years ago.'

'Oh. Why did you leave university?'

'For several reasons. But to tell the truth, I suppose I wanted to prove that some of those who teach can also do.'

'Did you publish anything?'

'Heaps—and I did collaborate on several papers. Probably the most famous is Jackson and Smith's *Preferred Structures for Computer Based Training Modules*.'

'That rings a bell. Of course I have heard of it—so you are that Smith. That was an excellent paper. Look, you must come and address the next meeting of the State Personnel Managers Society. I'm the current president. We will have to postpone the planned talk but don't you worry about that.'

Just then the telephone rang.

Ms Lion pressed the hands-free button.

'Yes, Susan.'

'It's Mr Counter, Head of Financial Administration. He says it's urgent.'

'This better be serious, Mr Counter. I am in the middle of an important meeting.' A few minutes of company discussion then followed between Ms Lion and Mr Counter. She hung up and returned to me.

'I shouldn't tell you this and be a tattletale but last week he missed a very important heads of department meeting I called about introducing a new personnel policy. He will live to regret that snub I promise you.'

I nodded understandingly.

'Well, Mr Smith, in your opinion exactly what help do you consider your company can provide for my organisation?'

Profile of a Politician

In the same way that the Mover is the antithesis of the Doublechecker, so the Politician is the opposite of the Artist. Verbal rather than visual, Politicians tend to have fixed opinions that they aggressively force on others. Unfortunately Ps can be so competitive in social discourse that they sometimes appear boastful and conceited. As these are not popular traits, Politicians who lack a strong Normal component can offend their colleagues. If they have a limited desire for social approval and lack self-control, Politicians will respond with more aggression and truculence in the face of social censure. However, if the Politician has good self-control, the desire to win often results in leadership.

The Artist tends to avoid social gatherings and if forced to attend may retreat into a shell. By contrast, Politicians, who love any form of games or sport, prefer those social contacts which they consider will provide an opportunity to engage in competitive conversations and discussions.

The language of the Politician centres around auditory words. Below are some examples:

'I hear you loud and clear ...'

'That name rings a bell with me.'

'That project sounds interesting.'

'Now listen carefully to what I am going to say.'

'The problem with most managers is their inability to communicate.'

These words: 'discuss, rings, sounds, listen, say, tell, and communicate' are auditory and orientated towards sounds. The dominant use of 'sound' words in conversation is a good indicator of the Politician component.

You can quickly recognise the self-importance of Politicians; they generally keep you waiting for an appointment. The desk in the office of a Politician is often placed diagonally in the far corner from the entrance to the office or in a dominant position. Degrees, awards, and pictures of teams with the Politician in the centre as captain frequently hang on the office walls. Ps tend to be formal and not use first names unless they also have a strong Mover or Hustler component.

> "You can always tell a Politician, but you cannot tell him much."

Once they give an opinion or an instruction Politicians so want to win and so hate to lose that they often stick stubbornly to their initial statement. I especially remember one example of the mulish behaviour of a Politician CEO during a management meeting. Before the meeting started he instructed his personal assistant to hold all telephone calls. Halfway through the meeting the telephone on his desk began to ring. He continued to talk, letting the telephone ring and ring. After at least five minutes when all around him were desperate to pick up the telephone the ringing finally stopped. The Politician acted as if nothing unusual had happened and continued talking about what he had achieved as a CEO over the past five years.

Politicians naturally have a high opinion of themselves. Their conversation is egocentric. 'I'll tell you what I think' and 'I said' are frequent phrases. Often their opinions are not only fixed but also biased. When two Ps meet it can be almost biblical—it is very often a case of an I for an I.

Ps enjoy arguments and discussions, which they often win because they are good at expressing themselves. They interpret facts to suit themselves and can be tenacious and stubborn in their beliefs. The Pope who conferred infallibility on himself was a true Politician. As a perceptive aphorist once said: 'You can always tell a Politician, but you cannot tell him much.'

Politicians often adopt another person's ideas and then use them as their own. Civil servants over time become very good at using this trait to introduce new plans or projects.

The self-righteousness of the Politician can be very irritating to other people. Politicians often give unsolicited advice and make comments about issues that do not concern them. Because of their strong desire to win, they strive to gain positions that will improve their status and prestige.

Unfortunately organisations sometimes promote Politicians above their competence (the Peter Principle) and the Politician becomes bossy and domineering towards everyone reporting to them. They resent any questioning of their authority and antagonistic arguments may follow. A Politician in this position habitually talks about lines of authority and then either breaks or disregards them.

Ps do not only like to win, they like to show other people that they have won. They hanker after signs of authority. Just as the South American dictators have medals emblazoned on their chests, the business card of a Politician usually contains a string of letters. Politicians need respect and admiration and believe such trappings help them. Unfortunately, they can become suspicious of their colleagues and a mild form of paranoia may set in. Office memos and emails may start to flow, as the Politician is good at office warfare. The Politician may become increasingly impervious to reason, maintaining that counter-arguments are false. He or she might end up believing that everyone else is wrong and too dumb to understand the 'truth'.

Because they hate to lose, Politicians are good at shifting blame to other people if mistakes occur. They will hold a grudge for a long time. If forced to do something against their wishes by someone in higher authority Politicians will often do the task unwillingly and under protest.

Not only do Politicians want signs of authority, they want positions of authority. They will join clubs and soon try to run the whole show. Unlike the Mover, who craves the social contact, Politicians regard organisations as another game and the person who gets to the top as the winner.

Because they are capable of supporting bizarre causes, Politicians can transform society. Their absolute confidence in their own beliefs and intolerance of opposing views means that they are often in the vanguard of change in society. On the other hand, their need for status and power often means that Politicians join intrinsically conservative organisations such as the armed forces or the police so that they can exercise authority. Politicians often become the chief executives of large organisations and unions.

One classic Politician stereotype is the left-wing shop steward who is suspicious of any proposition made by management. Politicians are also common in government: think of a Prime Minister or a President and you are usually thinking of a Politician.

A leader's personality should contain a lot of the Politician component. Without it, the instability in decision-making would be too disruptive. The stable opinions of the Politician, which he or she can usually state forcefully and with self-assurance, are most important to organisational development. This is because organisations will often succeed if they have goals and stick to them; it often does not matter whether the goals are optimal. Even if defeated several times, Politicians will persistently keep returning to the battle, and this is what makes them so competitive in sport, politics and business.

If, however, the Politician lacks self-control and maturity, he or she may be a problem as a leader. Those reporting to him may argue and then leave. The departures will be bitter and cause resentment and concern to those still reporting to the Politician. Politicians can sometimes tend to be too domineering in employee relationships and people often accuse them of being little dictators. Ps tend to take personal credit for the successes of their department but ensure that failures are shared co-operatively or blamed on an underling.

The person with little Politician component is a good follower, unprejudiced and compliant. There is no fear of a person with low Politician component leading a coup d'etat. Indeed, if low Politicians are put in positions of authority they may prove failures as they will vacillate over decisions and fail to inspire those beneath them. Faced with even mild opposition, they will crumble. They lack the competitive spirit which management requires. It is easy to deflect low Ps from current tasks and they often fail to follow through on work started.

The clothing of Politicians is generally nondescript but of good quality; if possible they like to buy the best they can afford. Blue is one of their favourite colours which is also the colour of many political parties. With regard to accessories, they're not ostentatious. They use good quality brand names, but again, tend to follow the norms of the organisation for whom they work. If there is anything to be said about the dress of Politicians it is that they do tend to like uniforms or work in organisations that are large and have uniforms for the workers. With regard to hobbies and social activities, they love team sports, particularly ones that are competitive. They drive powerful cars which have status. Politicians like, for example, Mercedes. Indeed the metallic blue Mercedes could be regarded the ideal car of a Politician.

The 1940s were the decade of the Politician. Dress commonly consisted of a uniform and the constant conflict and aggression of that decade is the behaviour typical of Politicians. Even when World War II was over it was followed by spy trials and purges on both sides. The most popular form of dancing was the jitterbug, which some contemporaries saw as being less of a dance and more of throwing your partner around the room.

What are the strengths of the Politician component in a personality? One is that Politicians have stable opinions and are not easily swayed. They also strive to prevent defeat. Politicians make good leaders, are forceful and decisive, and able to hold their own against opposition and don't quit until beaten. They're not frightened of supervising nor disciplining other people and in their own actions are assertive and self-assured.

On the other hand, as with the other components, Ps have weaknesses. They can be highly opinionated on certain subjects and will not listen to other reasonable beliefs that are put forward. They dig their heels in without necessarily having the facts first. Not only are they opinionated, they're also prickly. They give criticism but do not take it easily. Ps take offence if they feel they have been hard done by, they will harbour a grudge, and they have a long memory for insults. Politicians, when they do lose, take defeat in a hard way. Politician managers can be too domineering and unreasonable in their demands, and their stubborn actions may alienate subordinates or peers who become so distressed that they resign.

The Engineer

It is now time to discuss the third of the introvert temperament components, the Engineer. Engineers are people who are dominated by the desire to complete inspired projects. I have used the Engineer as a stereotype because that is how many engineers view their work—as builders of something useful that requires creative inspiration.

Engineers often become so possessed by what they are doing that they shut out the rest of the world. People who lack this characteristic of fierce concentration tend to regard Engineers as absent-minded and too theoretical, when they are in fact the most practical of all temperament types when it comes to completing a task. Engineers not only work in the construction industry but are also common in businesses where the work is project-orientated such as software, commercial law and product design. I have met many people with big Engineer components both when I was a software systems engineer with IBM and now as a venture capital investor in high technology companies with relatively large research and development departments.

Again the prospect in this cameo, Mr Barry Beaver, is an amalgamation of several people. The beaver is an animal that spends all its life building dams and lake dwellings. A beaver will always complete a dam once it starts to build one, and once built the dam never breaks.

First meeting with an Engineer

McIntosh & Jones was a leading industrial project design company specialising in chemical process plants. The head office was located in a low modern building in a new industrial estate set back among the trees. I was to see Mr

Barry Beaver, the chief engineering manager, to discuss the support needed following the purchase of a new flatbed plotter our company had developed.

I arrived five minutes early. The reception area contained several models of refineries and chemical plants. There were also at least twenty photographs of various manufacturing plants neatly and evenly spaced on the walls.

The receptionist buzzed Mr Beaver and I was given a plastic visitor's badge and told to proceed to the top level where Mr Beaver was waiting for me. He was of medium build with short hair and glasses. His shirtsleeves were rolled up to the elbow. There was a row of coloured pens and pencils in the left hand pocket of his shirt. His tie was a simple blue and green striped pattern.

> We shook hands.
>
> 'Mr Beaver?'
>
> 'Yes. Call me Barry. Look, I'm sorry, the receptionist told me your name but I was involved with something else when she rang. I've forgotten your name.'
>
> 'Smith. Jim Smith,' I said as I handed across a card.
>
> He looked at it for moment then turned suddenly and started walking.
>
> 'Come on, let's get going. Time is money, you know.'
>
> We arrived at his office, which was at the end of the corridor, and he ushered me in. I don't think I have ever seen an office more crammed with books and paper. One wall contained a bookshelf, which reached from floor to ceiling, and which was packed with books. On the opposite wall he had pinned a large planning chart, which was full of arrows and activities, alongside a whiteboard. The whiteboard was also filled with figures, drawings and equations.
>
> We sat down at his desk, which was packed with piles of files and working papers and the latest personal computer. He opened a drawer, rummaged around and, with a triumphant smile, produced a business card.
>
> 'I knew a packet of cards was in there. Everyone chips me about my desk but I know where everything is. I find it unbearable when our office manager tries to tidy it up.'
>
> By now I was beginning to notice the flat, dry tone of Barry's voice. It reminded me of the voice synthesisers you hear in modern lifts or computer-based voice response systems. Just then the phone rang.
>
> 'Excuse me, Jim,' he said as he picked up the phone. 'Yes … what do you mean the DVDs haven't arrived? That's impossible, damn it!'
>
> For the first time Barry's voice rose—he was definitely annoyed.

'This is the third time in a fortnight we have been promised these DVDs—we need that latest software release and the new training courses and manuals. This is the final straw. We are never going to buy anything from that computer company again. I want you to get in touch with their CEO every half hour until we have those DVDs. The delay's killing us—we've got ten drafting staff and three design engineers hanging around doing nothing and we've slipped three weeks down the critical path. We can't afford the cost or the time slippage.'

He slammed down the phone and several pieces of plastic shot into the air.

'Damn, I think I broke the telephone.'

'Well, that's easily fixed.'

'Yes but it's a hassle.'

'What's the problem?'

'Oh it's to do with a new project we are working on. I had decided it was time to upgrade our engineering design systems with new CAD workstations. They were meant to be compatible with the old ones. Well, they're not and our database of drawings is inaccessible. Everyone was really enthusiastic about the new stations. The exterior design is good. Now we are beginning to wonder if we made a mistake.'

There was a knock at the door.

'Yes.'

'Your phone doesn't appear to be working, Mr Beaver.'

'Oh yes. Come in, Jane.' She walked in carrying a glass of water and a packet of Alka-Seltzer.

'How many?'

'Two, I think, Jane, thank you.'

She dropped two tablets in the water and walked out. As the tablets started to effervesce Barry began to talk.

'We had our annual local Engineering Society dinner last night and we all drank a little too much wine. I don't generally drink to excess but you have to let your hair down occasionally. I must admit I can't remember the taxi ride home nor getting into bed.'

'Well, a good night recharges the batteries.'

'Absolutely—now, what exactly is the implementation and support plan for our new flat bed plotter? I don't want the same stuff-ups I am having with our new CAD stations.'

Profile of the Engineer

Engineers (or Es) are driven by the desire to complete projects. Es must complete the project they are working on. Engineers are highly achievement-oriented and they need goals. However, Engineers are practical and generally reject anything that is too far-fetched. Engineers are conscientious and meticulous about following through on detail. They can become immersed in minor matters and become fussy. However when Es complete a project, they derive tremendous satisfaction on achieving the task. While working on a project, they can be impatient under the pressure of time or cost and irritable about interruptions. They particularly dislike, once they've set out their plan, to have any changes to it. Engineers are single-minded, they cannot work on multiple projects. Their motto is one thing at a time, get it done and do it well.

Their clothing is interesting. It's generally immaculate and clean but slightly unusual in its colouring. It doesn't quite mix and match. Es often have pens in their pocket, ready to complete the next task or write down some detail they may have overlooked. Es love gadgets and devices and they know how they all work. They are the first to own PDAs and will buy the latest mobile phone if it has a new technical feature. They are the one wearing the latest Bluetooth earpiece. They like hobbies that require them to learn the detail about their interest. They go in for solitary occupations like collecting stamps, or coins, or working on computers.

> "Es devote great attention to detail and their crammed bookshelves are usually a good clue to their personality."

The office of an Engineer is easy to recognise by the filled bookcase and the project control chart on the wall. The desk is not always neat but the Engineer knows where everything is. They can become upset if they find their office or working area changed or altered. Although they are plodding, deliberate and thorough, Engineers are very enthusiastic when inspired.

Engineers are active people who like to be outdoors. They like to play sport and are the ones who are often seen jogging around the roads and parks in the mornings, lunchtimes or evenings. When in the office Es stand up and stretch often. Another characteristic of Engineers is their prodigious drinking about which they frequently reminisce, especially when they were at university. Nevertheless as they get older their tendency to drink combined with less exercise often leads to the Engineer being overweight. Es also often have hobbies that involve building or testing things and they are often the first people to try a new product.

Engineers prefer to do one thing at a time in an orderly fashion. They spend their time creating projects and then completing them. If the project is sufficiently inspiring the Engineer can go into ecstasy and the resulting task can be so burned into the personality that it becomes a dominating influence. The Engineer will then attack the task with a doggedness that may ensure success but can also result in a blind obsession.

If Engineers become frustrated in doing a task, they can become tense and upset. They become complaining, fussy people who may suddenly explode—indeed their frustration can sometimes transform itself into violent physical rages. This irritability causes Engineers to be loners—they tend to try to complete projects themselves and find it difficult to delegate responsibility.

As stated before, Engineers are deliberate and single-minded and dislike interruption. They love to read about a subject thoroughly. Es devote great attention to detail and their crammed bookshelves are usually a good clue to their personality. Another clue is their monotonous tone of voice in conversation—Engineers tend to be pedantic and to go on and on about the same topic, which may drive their listeners into a coma-like submission. Their conversation is often self-centred and they love to talk about their achievements. These achievements may be impressive if the Engineer component is allied to some talent or intelligence. Some great figures in history, such as Alexander the Great, Julius Caesar and Mohammed, are examples of Engineer-dominated personalities. If the Engineer is an individual of scant intelligence or talent, then the personality can appear over-fussy and difficult. Another clue is that Engineers have strong likes and dislikes. However, unlike the Politician and the Artist, you can sway these opinions by the force of either inspired or detailed argument.

Engineers like to test or trial a product or service before they buy, and prefer to get involved physically with it. This desire to get information by feeling the product and desire for activity is reflected in their language. The language of the Engineer is peppered with action and feeling words; they are tactile and like things to be tangible.

'I don't feel warm about the project.'

'Lay your cards on the table and give me some concrete examples.'

'Before I embrace your idea I have to get some sense of the risks involved and make sure there is a plan in place for a smooth implementation.'

'To push this proposal through I will have to pull some strings.'

The 1950s was the Engineers' decade. These were the years of great scientific projects such as the H-Bomb, satellites in space and vaccines based on thorough testing. Some people called the 1950s the 'sleeping decade' because of the placid, non-revolutionary behaviour of the students.

Green, particularly in England, is the colour of the Engineer. British Racing Green is the colour in which British sports cars race. Their cars are like Swiss clocks that run well and efficiently. Engineers buy well-engineered cars or engineering classics. The green BMW or green Jaguar is often a good indicator of an Engineer.

Many of the leaders of the 'green' environment movement have personalities with dominant or influential Engineer component. Engineers enjoy activities, which combine the outdoors, completion of a task, and solitude, such as bushwalking, rock climbing, or canoeing. A major reason for the success of the 'green' movement is the dedication and persistence of its leaders and these are two of the characteristics of the Engineer.

People weak in the Engineer component tend to be careless and bored with repetitive work. People generally criticise low Engineers for not being persistent and objective enough. People with low Engineer component have limited powers of analysis and tend to diffuse themselves over many tasks. Low Es dislike planning and tend to behave in a reactive fashion.

Engineers are good workers, they're meticulous and they're careful and they gain satisfaction out of work that others may regard as being monotonous. They're systematic in their approach and methodical in their operation, and above all, they have the persistence to finish what they start. There are, of course, some weaknesses with the Engineer component, for they may get so caught up in the details that they lose touch with their immediate objective. Also, they may end up devoting excessive time to an impractical project. Their fussiness may annoy others. They are also not good at delegating responsibility, and once they have completed something and they like the way it is done, they're resistant to change and can become entrenched in their ways.

The Hustler

We now return to the last of the extrovert components—the Hustler. The Hustler stereotype is an individual driven solely by a desire for material success. Few people are completely devoid of a desire for wealth—most of us have at some time wanted a new car or a new item of clothing.

Indeed, much of modern advertising is directed towards stimulating this desire, so it is not surprising that it is so prevalent.

Middlemen and brokers need to have a lot of Hustler in order to succeed. I have worked for nine years in the financial services industry and have met many brokers. Stockbrokers live by commission and have to create a market. To the questions 'Should I sell?' and 'Should I buy?' the broker must answer yes in both instances. Brokers are sometimes accused of being two-faced; to pay the alimony they have to be.

In the short sketch that follows I have chosen as a prospect a real estate agent, who is a composite of several people I know. I have called him Mr Frederick Fox, since, traditionally, the fox is a shrewd, crafty character. I am sure that you, like me, will be familiar with several people who have some Hustler influence in their personality.

First meeting with a Hustler

I was on my way to see Fox & Crow, real estate agents located in the main street. My appointment was with Frederick Fox, whom I understood to be the general manager. Our company was considering whether to open a new branch office and I had been given the project of finding a suitable site. I managed to find a parking space down the street from their office and as I walked towards it I could not help noticing how their bright yellow and red sign stood out from the rest.

I walked in. The receptionist was a tinted blonde wearing a tight, red, sleeveless dress over a good figure. She had a deep tan and was wearing gold bracelets on both arms and rings on three fingers of each hand. She gave me a warm, friendly smile and when I introduced myself said, 'Ah yes, sit down. Mr Fox is expecting you.'

I sat down on the red, yellow and brown lounge with my eyes slightly squinting from the burnished orange carpet. Right on time, Mr Fox strolled into the reception area.

'Jim, isn't it?' he said as he extended his hand and also gave me a warm and friendly smile.

'Yes, Mr Fox,' I said shaking his hand. His handshake was firm and slightly prolonged.

'No, no, everyone calls me Fred. He looked down at my card. Isn't Ted Tiger your MD? I played golf with him several weeks ago. He is a great guy.'

I nodded.

'Come this way into my office. It's at the back where I like it. This way I have to walk backwards and forwards past the staff and I can see who's working and who's playing around.'

We went into the main office and as he closed the door he put his arm around my shoulder and murmured, 'Mind you, I wouldn't mind playing around with that receptionist.'

I nodded in agreement, perhaps a little too vigorously and hastily.

On the way through the main office Fred caught me looking at the sales commission board.

'Those are our quarterly budgets. Besides the standard commissions we have our own special competition. The one at the top gets to take their partner out to the best restaurant in town—the one at the bottom becomes externally redeployed.'

'We have something similar at our office.'

'Oh, yes, and what position are you?'

'Oh, at the top,' I replied, somewhat stretching the truth as our competition had only started that week and nobody had runs on the board.

'Good. I only like to work with winners.'

Just before we entered Mr Fox's office a salesman yelled out, 'Fred. Fine Cotton came in at six to one!'

'Terrific—that's $300. You play the sport of kings, Jim?'

'Occasionally. Fine Cotton? Where have I heard that name before?'

'Oh, it's a famous horse that was substituted in a big race in Brisbane about nine months ago. Fine Cotton is a country hacker. Well, I got the inside dope so I backed in on the tote so I wouldn't have any bookies chasing me for a refund if the switch was found out. It's beautiful—I have now made money on both the real Fine Cotton and the false one.'

We both laughed as we sat down. Fred's desk was neat and tidy. There were two pictures on the desk. One was of two kids and no wife. The other was of Fred shaking hands with an older gentleman and receiving a plaque. Under the second photograph was the notation 'Best Salesman in the Country 2006'. On one wall was a poster saying 'Money is not everything, but it sure comes a close second to whatever is.'

There was a moment's silence as we sized each other up. Fred was wearing a grey suit, which had a slightly glittering thread running through it and a bright red striped tie with a designer label. On his left wrist was what looked like a Cartier watch and on his right a chunky gold bracelet. He was also wearing tinted glasses.

Behind him on the wall was a big oil painting that looked like a Johnson, one of the better known modern artists being talked about in the Sunday paper's arts pages. I looked at the painting but could not see the distinctive Johnson signature which was always placed in the top left corner. Fred saw my eyes looking at the painting.

'What do you think?'

'Well,' I said, 'It looks like a Johnson but I can't ...'

'Can't see the signature—well it's an original copy. I had a local artist do it for me.'

'Ah that explains it—uh, it's very good.'

'Yeah—Johnson was my ex-wife's favourite painter. Still this talk isn't making either of us any money. Now what is your budget for rental?'

Profile of the Hustler

In this section we cover the component dominated by the desire for material success. We call this stereotype the Hustler. The Hustler is like a fox, sly and cunning, and ambitious for material and financial gain. Hustlers are generally concerned with self-advantage. They listen to one radio station, WIIFM (What's In It For Me). They take risks for quick gains, love to gamble, and see themselves as astute and shrewd. If you need their co-operation, remember: Hustlers do not like doing something for nothing.

Hustlers have friendly, genial smiles. Of all the stereotypes Hustlers (or Hs) are the most charming and certainly the most entertaining company. Hustlers maintain constant eye contact—they never look away. Some have subconsciously realised that their penetrating eyes cause discomfort so they tend to wear dark or tinted glasses, even indoors. Hustlers soon give themselves away in conversation, often telling stories about their contacts with celebrities. They tend to use first names early, both that of the person they are talking to and any name they think will impress. Hustlers are name-droppers and social climbers so they pepper their conversation with the names of the latest restaurants, shows, people, and so on. Their conversation is as smooth as a television talk show. Note that Hustlers are excellent actors—they are flexible and can adapt themselves to most situations, and because of this they often gain early popularity.

Hustlers like to display and talk about their success. Hs believe that money won is twice as pleasant as money earned and money will soon crop up in their conversations. Often the story is how they have made some quick, fast capital gains in the past year. Hs believe that making money is easy so this emphasis in conversation is not surprising. Hustlers also tend to be gamblers and love going to horse races, casinos and dog races. Anecdotes about their own gambling successes and others' failures crop up often in their conversation. Hustlers enjoy telling stories, particularly about incidents that present them in a favourable light.

> "Hustlers are generally concerned with self-advantage. They listen to one radio station, WIIFM (What's In It For Me)."

Their clothing is generally ostentatious. Hustlers like gold and reds. Hustler men generally wear red or red-striped ties and they have gold bracelets, gold chains hung around the neck, unbuttoned shirts and showy gold watches. The women wear lots of gold accessories as well. Their clothes look expensive and designer label even if they're not. Hs are flashy and showy; Hustler women with attractive legs will wear mini-skirts.

With regard to hobbies, Hustlers like exciting activities such as skiing. They're not in fact 'hobby people'—they're not the sort to be prone to sitting down and quietly working away collecting stamps or painting or drawing, or doing home study unless they think it will help them to improve their financial standing. What they want to do are activities such as boat racing and polo where they're around and mixing with other people who they regard as winners in life. Horse racing is another activity that satisfies their need for excitement and gambling.

Hustlers like cars are that fast and showy. The red Porsche and Ferrari (or gold metallic Mercedes) are classic cars driven by the Hustler. The decade of the Hustler was the late 1970s and early 1980s when 'Greed was good.'

Hustlers often tend to take a robust view of the law. They tend to go as close as they can to breaking it without doing so. They always drive just over the speed limit. Hustlers will spend much time analysing rules so that they can bend them to their advantage. The irony is if the reverse happens and a Hustler is caught out on some technicality then he or she will go on and on about other people's imperfections and lack of ethics. Hustlers closely follow the letter of the law but often forget the spirit. When the Hustler says, 'I am going to be perfectly honest with you,' be on your guard, especially if he or she then goes on to describe how someone else is going to break the rules or be deceptive. You should be careful not to be taken for a ride.

Because they are charming and affable Hustlers make friends easily. The friendships may be short-lived, however, because other people may become tired of their emphasis on material objects. Sometimes Hustlers with low Normal prove to be untrustworthy and they are often snobs. The streak of snobbery manifests itself particularly in restaurants and hotels where Hustlers tend to treat the staff as members of a lower class. Hustlers divide the world into winners and losers. Hustlers are oblivious to the losers and flatter the winners. Hustlers will fawn over and pander to those they think are higher in status than themselves, especially if they think such actions will help them climb the social ladder. As a result Hustlers sometimes seem sycophantic in the presence of their superiors.

Hustlers often divorce as they have generally married for the wrong reasons. Typically the Hustler appeals to the future spouse's maternal or paternal instinct, rather than the marriage stemming from both parties wanting to form a mutual partnership. The spouse gets a divorce when the Hustler either has an affair or is felt not to be contributing fairly to the relationship. The divorce proceedings are usually long and drawn out because Hustlers are good at shedding crocodile tears, circumventing any blame and eliciting sympathy.

Hustlers are good opportunists, charming and very conscious of money—especially other people's. If they are intelligent and have lots of self-control they become successful businesspeople.

Hustlers are common in the upper echelons of business and government. They often make good salespeople as they are good at ingratiating themselves with prospects and show finesse. Hs are often promoted, but they find it difficult to be a first-level line manager because the other staff perceive them as superficial and lacking depth. Frustrated, the Hustler generally moves to a higher position with a competitor. Hustlers are egocentric—they are most loyal to themselves.

Low Hustlers are most commonly found in public service institutions such as hospitals or social welfare. These people want to sacrifice themselves for others. They are uninterested in money; they are sometimes so over-generous that they become painful to their colleagues. Sometimes the deficiency is so great that the low Hustler suffers from the martyr complex. An example of the martyr complex is the mother who centres all her interest on her children with the expectation of total support when the children reach maturity.

Low Hustlers are generally long-term, loyal employees but sometimes, after a long period of work, honestly believe that the company should completely support them, regardless of current performance. So, in a strange way, a person completely lacking in Hustler and a person totally dominated by it can have the similar belief that the world owes them a living.

The Hustler divides the world up into winners and losers. The winners are a small group of people who are 'in-the-know', shrewd, opportunistic and have made it to the top by taking risks and manipulating other people who they regard as weak and losers. Hustlers believe that the best way to achieve wealth is to use the techniques they learned as small children: charming comments, winning smiles and occasional emotional tantrums. Indeed much of the attraction of the Hustler is due to his or her childlike charm.

Charles Dickens provided this great quote in *Oliver Twist*, spoken by Fagin, who is one of the great Hustlers of literature. 'Some conjurors say that number three is the magic number, and some say number seven. It's neither, my friend, neither. It's number one.'

Hustlers are typically middlemen. They like working in occupations where they deal with people and they stand in between buyers and sellers. You find them in a variety of industries that deal with secondary markets, ranging from real estate agents to car dealers to merchant banks. If you are dealing with an individual who is a middleman, earning his commission from either the buyer or the seller, where the rewards can be large, it is likely that the Hustler is dominant. A good example would be Los Angeles and the movie industry where one is dealing with the concepts and you have to put various parties together. As is well known, the typical Hollywood agent drives a red Porsche, wears sunglasses, lots of gold and a genial smile and name drops all the time.

Hustlers will work very hard if they perceive they are going to be rewarded financially. Hustlers make things happen. Hustlers generally help businesses succeed through overcoming the competition and working for their joint self-interest. If they are working in a group or a company that provides them with material success they can be fiercely loyal.

On the other hand Hustlers rarely have stable job histories. This is a weakness of the Hustler. They generally cannot hold the same job for too long. They get bored with it, they see greater financial opportunity elsewhere and then they go and grab it. The grass is often perceived to the Hustler as being greener on the other hills. They will suddenly be tempted by the offer of more money and status and will suddenly move to a competitor.

The Normal

Normals are driven by the desire for order. To achieve order Normals (or Ns) know that they must adjust their behaviour to the expectations of their colleagues. Those lacking in Normal would consider the behaviour that Normals consider natural as conformist. Normals are concerned about ethics and consequently often work in professions such as law and accounting. We have chosen an accountant as the Normal stereotype in the cameo that follows. We have called our accountant Ms Pauline Penguin. This is because the black and white formality of the penguin so reflects the controlled nature of the Normal. Black, white and grey—particularly charcoal greys—are the colours of the Normal. Ns often wear white shirts, charcoal grey suits and discreet ties. Just as penguins gather in flocks, so do Normals, who prefer to work in large organisations that have standards, policies and traditions. We have all met people with big N components. Your parents and older relatives will usually be high Normals.

First meeting with a Normal

DMG Sanderson was one of the big ten accounting firms. Recently the professional body regulating the accountants had decided to allow advertising. I was an account executive for a local advertising agency (known as 'a suit' by the creative staff all whom wore baggy trousers and casual tops) and a telemarketing campaign had secured several appointments. I was to see Pauline Penguin, the partner responsible for administration.

I arrived at the office five minutes early. The offices were mahogany and had discreet grey carpets. The receptionist was conservatively dressed and had a beautifully modulated English accent. I was asked to sit down. On the table were the standard society journals and business magazines. Right on time a younger woman stepped into the foyer. She was in neat black suit and white shirt. She was wearing black court shoes, conservative jewellery and an expensive watch. Her hair was extremely well-groomed and her make-up was discreet.

> "Increasing age results in a more balanced personality, less likely to show emotional extremes. This change of personality as one becomes more mature and integrated into society is the development of the Normal component."

'Jim Smith?' she said, extending her hand.

'Yes. Pauline Penguin, I presume.' We both laughed slightly as we shook hands.

'Thank you for coming in. I have arranged for some other people to meet with us. Come along to the board room.'

We proceeded down the hall to a room with a large boardroom table at which several people were sitting. They were all wearing blue pin-striped suits, white shirts and conservative ties except for one. He was wearing a grey suit, a pale blue shirt and a striped tie. The three blue pin-stripes were the senior audit, tax, and consulting partners while the grey suit was Mr Jones, a recently appointed public relations consultant.

After shaking hands and introducing ourselves we all sat down. We then handed around business cards. 'Just like the Japanese,' one of the partners commented. We all gave a slight laugh.

'Well I guess it's my turn to be in the chair,' said Ms Penguin.

'I have had an agenda produced so I suppose we should begin with that. Here, everyone, have a copy.' All of us studied the agenda.

'Any requests for changes? No? Well let's begin. Before I proceed however, I think
I should inform you, Mr Smith, that every decision in this practice has to be one of total agreement among the four of us. We have asked Mr Jones along because he is an expert in this area and he has said it is important for promotional efforts to be coordinated.

'Oh, I agree.'

'Yes, we thought the point had logical appeal.'

'Item 1 on the agenda is a brief introduction to our company. That onerous task falls on to me. Essentially DMG Sanderson is one of the oldest audit practices in the world. We are not the biggest but we think we are the best. We are particularly good at hiring people from outside the company and, by a process of mutual interaction, developing new business areas. For example, our consulting division was the first in this city associated with an accounting firm and is still regarded as the best.

'We know little about advertising and it has been a matter of some debate at the last full partners' meeting whether we should spend hard-earned fees on advertising. However, it was agreed to appoint a sub-committee that you see here and we have been empowered to run a trial campaign on a restricted budget.'

'Well I must agree that is logical.'

'Indeed. Suppose you tell us a little about your company. Do you have a company brochure?'

Profile of a Normal

If we compare the adult to the child we can think of several differences in behaviour. Children tend to cry or throw a tantrum when something goes wrong. Children tend to be far more emotional than adults and lack stability. As individuals mature they become more reserved and prudent. They desire order. Increasing age results in a more balanced personality, less likely to show emotional extremes. This change of personality as one becomes more mature and integrated into society is the development of the Normal component. The Normal component acts as a stabiliser on the other six components discussed so far. For example:

- The over-excitable and distracting Mover changes into a friendly, sociable, enthusiastic optimist.
- The insecure and procrastinating Doublechecker becomes a compassionate, cautious, conscientious and stable administrator.
- The detached and secretive Artist changes into a creative, imaginative, sensitive individual.
- The aggressive, arrogant Politician turns into a steadfast, decisive, forceful leader.
- The fussy preoccupied Engineer becomes a thorough, meticulous, and systematic project manager.
- The wheeler-dealer of the Hustler changes into the realistic, shrewd, astute acumen of the successful business executive.

If, as is common, the Normal is average to strong and combined with some other strong components then the individual is fortunate. The resulting combination is often a dynamic, powerful and integrated personality. The Normal both gives direction to and inhibits the other components.

The Normal acts as a veneer which society puts over the original personality of the individual. Ns tend to be people who follow the norms of the society in which they live. They observe the formal social courtesies; for example, they shake hands and exchange business cards early. They are punctual for appointments and dislike people who are late. They have tidy desks and have neat handwriting. Ns wear conservative clothes; for example the grey flannel suit of good quality is the uniform of the Normal man. At the start of a conversation the Normal appears reserved and inhibited.

Normals are calm and self-composed and appear to have a flat personality. Normals love to be part of a group and will use references to other people or precedents as support for an argument. They also prefer the use of logic to emotion—indeed if an emotional person is present Normals become uncomfortable.

Normals have a strong sense of morals; their conversation will be peppered with references to standards of conduct. The stereotype Normal is a professional such as a lawyer or accountant. The Normal is sometimes perfectionist and dislikes finding mistakes in a proposal. Ns tend to call in experts and obtain a group approval for an idea. Classic Normal behaviour at the end of a meeting is to summarise the main points and suggest an action plan.

The Normal is very much into self-improvement. Normals attend the evening and part-time courses offered by various institutions and buy the how-to books sold in bookshops everywhere. The Normal practises persistently. The sport of the Normal is golf, which consists of learning an artificial swing and is dominated by individuals who practise incessantly. Golf with its rules and formal social courtesies is the classic Normal game and top golfers typically regard themselves as players who display much self-control.

Normals like to consider themselves as self-reliant and self-disciplined. Ns prefer individuals who stand on their own feet and who show the same emotional control as themselves. They are persistent when facing difficulties and exude a quiet confidence. The stereotypical English person is a good example of the Normal component. The Normal tends to be uncomplaining when faced with physical difficulties and shows a 'stiff upper lip'.

Along with their desire for order Normals respect the social norms. Tact, social mindfulness and respect for the privacy of another individual are all manifestations of the Normal desire for order. A basic goodness and charity towards other people, tempered with the need to follow social conventions, pervades the Normal personality. It is not surprising that England and Switzerland, which are among the most Normal countries, have founded many of the world's charities and have been frequent originators of philanthropic and nursing organisations such as the Red Cross.

A person with high Normal will tend to prefer cars that are esteemed for quality and have wide approval, such as a Mercedes, Jaguar or Rolls Royce. They will generally choose colours such as white, black or grey. The 1990s with its increasing conservatism, shift to political correctness and increased rules and regulations was the decade of the Normal.

People who have high Normal without any other strong component appear as unbending, rigid conservatives. People often accuse high Normals of being cold and colourless. High Normals demand high standards from others and they believe in both the letter and the spirit of the law. Their demands for high standards usually extend to their children and the result is often a conflict between parent and child. The same problem can occur in companies where a rigid orthodoxy of behaviour alienates new employees and causes the radicals to leave early so that only the more conventional stay. An organisation must adapt to its environment to survive, so the loss of the people who are most likely to come up with creative solutions to problems of change can prove fatal. Strong Normals are self-reliant; in a perverse way this characteristic may lead to difficulties when solutions need to be obtained by a group.

Weak Normals have no control over any dominant component and the condition can lead to mental illness if associated with an extreme of one of the other six components. If no other component is dominant the weak Normal will appear an unbalanced, uncontrolled individual. The conversation is often inconsistent and irrational and the individual is likely to break down under pressure.

A particularly dangerous combination is someone who has very high Hustler combined with very low Normal. This is the personality of a sociopath, i.e. people who are interested only in their personal needs and desires, without concern for the effects of their behaviour on others. These are the people who commit crimes. David Farrington's study of every male born in Britain in 1956 found that while around one-third had been convicted of at least one non-traffic offence only 5% were responsible for over half the crime committed by the 1956 cohort. Typically there are two groups of adolescent criminals. Around 85% gradually stop committing offences as their N develops. The remaining 15% continue to commit violent crimes over their lifetime. Research is beginning to show that the anti-social behaviour of the remaining group may be genetically determined.

Another dangerous combination is someone with a very high Politician combined with a very low Normal. This is the profile of workplace bullies who have a need to dominate and believe they can be popular or gain status through the dominance of someone less powerful. You should advise possible victims of their behaviour that they need to collect documentation of all the incidents because sometimes the bullying can be covert and hard to prove. You need to avoid direct confrontation as that might encourage a bully to exercise power over you. A better approach is to try to find areas of agreement and to expand on these. Another technique is to say, 'I am sure you are not aware of the effect you have ...'

The Normal tends to increase as a person gets older but then the Normal may begin to weaken slowly as the individual approaches senility or the second childhood. If the Normal continues to weaken beyond the state of dotage, then madness may develop.

The Emotionally Intelligent Manager

Step 1: Self-Awareness

Goldman describes the first step in developing Emotional Intelligence as Self-Awareness, which he defines as understanding your underlying dominant emotions. We now have a technology, the Humm-Wadsworth methodology, for achieving this goal.

How do you learn your dominant and weak components? The best way is to complete the full Humm-Wadsworth questionnaire, which takes around an hour, and then meet for another one-hour interview with a trained psychologist from Chandler & Macleod, who owns the test copyright. The Chandler & Macleod website: www.chandlergroup.com.au, will contain the name of the nearest office. If one is not nearby you can contact the company and it will arrange for the personality questionnaire and interview to be given by a trained psychologist in a suitable environment.

On the website is also a simple 21 question quiz that you can completer online and it will send you back a simple explanation of your temperament. Naturally this test is simplistic and you can not expect the same level of accuracy as if you completed the full test. However it may provide a useful indication of your dominant components. Note that this quiz will indicate the dominant components within your own personality; it does not tell you how the strength of your components compares to the rest of the population. For example if all your components are weak compared to the rest of the population except for M and P which are average, then the quiz will say you have dominant M and P.

The alternative is to use a heuristic technique. For those unfamiliar with the term, what this means is that through experience we can develop a set of rules about a phenomenon. People who have read the chapters on the seven components will realise that there are various differing characteristics of the seven components including the way we dress and talk. Hence it is possible to devise a simple questionnaire which contains a series of rules for each of the seven components. A good technique is to complete the questionnaire with someone who knows you well, such as a close relative or partner.

Answer the questions quickly, spending no more than several seconds per line. The whole test should take no more than two minutes. Then complete the personality profile at the end of the test.

Normal	Yes	No
On time and observes social graces		
Conservative clothing		
Tidy desk, office and dress		
Self-composed and calm		
Logical way of talking		
Calls in experts and other people present		
Undue concern for precedent and approval		
Finishes with action plan		
Reserved manner and unemotional		
Strong sense of morals and ethics		
Yes scores out of 10		

Hustler	Yes	No
Immediately on first name terms and genial smile		
Ostentatious jewellery, flashy watch		
Glitzy clothes (red and oranges)		
Name dropper and cheaper designer labels		
Constant eye contact		
Charming manner		
Egocentric		
Gambler or risk taker		
Interested in money and seeks discount		
Interested in 'wealthy' sports such as sailing, skiing and horseracing		
Yes scores out of 10		

Mover	Yes	No
Always late for appointment but apologises		
Immediately uses first names		
Smiles a lot, speaks energetically, tells jokes		
Dress is casual, colourful and humorous		
Mickey Mouse wristwatch, big jangling earrings		
Readily distracted by interruptions		
Big picture, not detail		
Untidy office, slogans on the wall		
Uses lots of hand gestures		
Lives a very active and full life, jogging in morning, clubbing at night		
Yes scores out of 10		

Doublechecker	Yes	No
Conservative hair style		
Earth colours in dress, beige, browns and greens		
Picture of family in office		
Office or handbag stuffed with files		
Likes to socialise before coming to business		
Hypochondriac		
Apologetic and indecisive		
Minor problems seem insurmountable		
Double-checks every feature of a proposal		
Avoids risky activities		
Yes scores out of 10		

Artist	Yes	No
No first names, no talk of family		
Avoids eye contact		
Shy and quiet		
Men have beards, women have long hair		
Sometimes stutter or stammer		
Hands over mouth pointing to eyes		
Non-egocentric		
Creative or oddball clothes and accessories		
Modern art in office		
Uses visual words		
Yes scores out of 10		

Politician	Yes	No
No first names		
Keeps you waiting, but does not apologise		
Quick on your title, position and importance		
Constant self-referral, egotistical		
Displays status symbols (degrees, pictures) in office		
Power dresser, blues and yellows		
Defends fixed opinions skillfully		
Uses auditory words		
Domineering, aggressive and truculent		
Plays competitive sports		
Yes scores out of 10		

Engineer	Yes	No
No first names		
Pens in pocket or glasses on chain		
Dress is clean and tidy, but does not match		
Details, not big picture		
Unemotional—yet suddenly enthusiastic about pet projects		
Monotonic voice level, but uses action words		
Office full of books, project timetable on wall		
Untidy desk or big full handbag		
Likes a drink		
Likes outdoor sports such as bush walking		
Yes scores out of 10		

Simply count the number of Yes answers for each component and fill in the column graph below. Seven or more Yes answers will indicate a strong component. Again, however, note that this quiz is simplistic and does not compare to the full test battery.

Component	N	H	M	D	A	P	E
10							
9							
8							
7							
6							
5							
4							
3							
2							
1							
0							

Sample Quick Check-List Graph

Component	N	H	M	D	A	P	E
10							
9							
8							
7		✔				✔	
6		✔	✔			✔	
5		✔	✔			✔	
4	✔	✔	✔		✔	✔	✔
3	✔	✔	✔		✔	✔	✔
2	✔	✔	✔	✔	✔	✔	✔
1	✔	✔	✔	✔	✔	✔	✔
0	✔	✔	✔	✔	✔	✔	✔

An investment banker specialising in corporate finance would have a personality profile similar to the above graph.

Step 2: Self-Management

The most sacred city of the ancient Greeks was Delphi, which is located in a valley of overpowering grandeur and solitude next to Mount Parnassus. It was the home of the famous Delphic oracle and was the centre of faith to the Greeks much as the Vatican today is for Catholics. The largest building in Delphi, the Great Temple of Apollo, housed the Omphalos. This was a stone, shaped like a half egg, which was believed by the Greeks to be the centre of the universe. Inscribed on the walls of the Great Temple were the two great commands of Greek life: *Know thyself* and *Everything in moderation.*

You have now had an introduction to the Humm-Wadsworth temperament technology. If you have completed the questionnaire in the previous chapter, you should have some understanding of your dominant and subordinate emotional drives. For many people this self-awareness is often their first step on the path developing emotional intelligence. Previously they suffered from a lack of a model of understanding people and so were unable to understand themselves. The transformation for most people when they first learn their dominant emotional drives is generally dramatic. For the first time in their lives they are able to follow the first Delphic commandment: *Know thyself.*

If you have completed the first step of self-analysis, you are now ready to take the second in the path of emotional intelligence: *Self-Management*. The first move is to learn what your *'hot buttons'* are. These are the behaviours or things that in the past would really upset you. Now you know when they happen to let them pass, saying to yourself, *'That's the bad side of my P drive working me up again. Keep calm, use it as a constructive force rather than one for self-destruction.'* In the next pages we have set out a list of hot buttons for each of the seven components. Learning this list could be one of the most useful things you do in life.

The key to successful Self-Management is to understand the second commandment of the Greeks: *Everything in moderation.* This command does not refer to some idealistic nirvana. Instead it is a process that never stops. It has two sides, controlling your strong drives and building up your weaker drives. The well-adjusted person is just that, a person who has moved all his or her emotional drives into the middle or optimal zone.

> "The key to successful Self-Management is to understand the second commandment of the Greeks: Everything in moderation."

To help you begin on your path of Self-Management, we have set out some habits and behaviours you can adopt to moderate your strong component. A good exercise is to examine your weak components and try to work out one or two things you can do to strengthen them without upsetting other people.

We all categorise people all the time. No one approaches anybody without doing some classification. We automatically see people as 'male or female', 'attractive or unattractive', 'friend or enemy', 'good or bad', etc. It is dishonest to think we don't do this. What is far better is to have a consistent and scientific model of behaviour to understand other people or ourselves. Using the Humm-Wadsworth model is actually liberating. First of all, you start to gain understanding of others—you begin to recognise behaviour that is the result of other people's dominant emotional drives. This behaviour would often in the past be upsetting to you because it conflicted with *your* dominant emotional drives. Now that you understand the model you have control over your behaviour and so take the second step on the path of developing emotional intelligence: Self-Management. You can say to yourself, *'I know what's happening here. This is a trivial matter. I don't worry about the small things in life, only the important ones. I will let this pass.'*

Hot buttons

Component	Behaviour that particularly aggravates this component
Normal	Criticising them. If you need to do so, make some excuse that says their mistake was atypical behaviour. Questioning their integrity. Acting inconsistently and being unpunctual.
Hustler	Ignoring them and being indifferent to the quality of their work. Looking down on them or trivialising their activities. Acting unprofessionally or being sloppy in work or play. Being secretive or evasive (they are sometimes and pick it up in a flash).
Mover	Restricting their freedom or their choices. Being pessimistic or negative. They hate nitpickers. Failing to react when they speak or come up with ideas. Refusing to pull your weight as a member of a team.
Doublechecker	Taking them for granted especially forgetting to thank them. Not including them in group activities or overlooking them. Trying to quickly introduce new ideas that may affect their security.
Artist	Making them the centre of attention. Being crude or insensitive; using loud behaviour. Ignoring their feelings or destroying their moods. Forcing them to be confrontational or aggressive.
Politician	Telling them what they can or cannot do. Trying to get the advantage over them even though they do it all the time with other people. Acting indecisively and not accepting responsibility.
Engineer	Acting or thinking emotionally particularly keeping a closed mind. Criticising their expertise and demonstrating incompetence yourself. Making surprise visits, giving them sudden tasks or monitoring them closely.

Some suggestions for Self-Development

Normal	Allow other people to be as they are and let them make decisions for themselves. Don't expect people to change immediately. Don't try to put order on your own irrationality. Not everyone is as objective as you are. Learn to relax. You cannot spend your whole time trying to fix the world. Remember the best you can do is good enough.
Hustler	Remember self-worth comes from within; not by chasing the approval of others. Give as much attention as you receive. Be truthful and ethical and stop trying to cut corners. Develop your spiritual side. Stop feeling jealous of others and having grandiose expectations of yourself.
Mover	Get into the habit of observing your impulses rather than acting on them immediately. Find ways of giving rather than getting. Fulfilment comes not from getting happiness but from relationships and seizing the moment. Going along with others all the time does not lead to good relationships. One-way communication only will fail.
Doublechecker	The greatest tragedy of all is to feel that at the end of your life you have missed the boat: Carpe diem. Don't be anxious about your anxieties. Remember anxiety can be energising. Resist the tendency to blame others and try some optimism. Don't try to build too much safety into your environment. Remember the only constant in the world is change. To the man who is afraid everything rustles.

Artist	Remember the more you seek peace of mind by avoiding conflict, the more likely you are to have conflict with others. Don't pay so much attention to your feelings especially your negative ones. Self-esteem comes from positive experiences. If you make a career of being different and trying to discover yourself, your self-indulgence will mean you never find yourself.
Politician	Remember the more you fight society's constraints and try to be independent the less likely you are to achieve your goals. Of all the types you can do the most harm and the most good. By which do you want to be remembered? Don't take action too quickly. You show real power when you show self-restraint and compassion.
Engineer	Learn to relax. Do this by exercise, not drinks or drugs. You are good at understanding things, use that understanding to identify with people. Share your feelings. Before you take constructive action, ask for advice from someone you trust.

Step 3: Social Awareness

The third step in developing Emotional Intelligence is generally defined as social awareness of other people or empathy. Understanding another person's emotional drives is the key to developing empathy. However, if you ask people who have high EQ how it is that have this skill, they typically reply that it comes naturally. In other words, it is an inborn talent rather than a learned skill. People, who have worked in sales positions, particularly where pay-for-performance represents a high proportion of the take home pay, have to develop empathy. If they do not, they usually fail.

> "Understanding another person's emotional drives is the key to developing empathy."

In this section we will describe a technique for analysing people according to six major behavioural clues. Using this technique you will gain some understanding of what the strongest emotional drivers of an individual are. The six clues we use are:

1. The way the individual talks,
2. The organisation the individual works for,
3. The individual's position in the organisation,
4. The individual's dress,
5. The individual's office or working environment,
6. The first meeting with an individual: are you kept waiting and how soon does the individual move to using first names.

As you gain familiarity with this technique you will start to see patterns in life and people where previously they did not exist. Your understanding of others should dramatically increase. Also as you remember that we all have the seven components inside us you learn to recognise not only the differences among people but also their similarities.

Talk

Talk is a most useful clue to the dominant components of a personality. Normals tend to talk logically and without emotion. Hustlers will name drop and bring up money early in the conversation. Movers have a lively, enthusiastic, smiling manner in contrast to Doublecheckers who are pessimistic and hypochondriacs complaining about invisible aches and pains. Artists are quiet, bashful and sensitive, and by contrast, Politicians are forceful, aggressive and opinionated. Engineers on the other hand come across as flat and monotonic in their speech.

Organisation

Organisations, as well as individuals, develop behavioural characteristics that determine their success in the business environment. For each type of industry it is possible to suggest which components will lead to organisational growth and development. These components will tend to become norms of behaviour. Norms refer to the standard of behaviour that is derived from the expectations of people both inside and outside the organisation. Good examples are such comments as 'X is a creative advertising agency' or 'Z is a marketing company'. People who have the expected norm as their dominant components will tend to succeed in those organisations. Each of the seven components can lead to success, depending on the organisation.

- The **Normal** component, with its emphasis on logic and precedent, tends to dominate professional organisations such as legal and accounting firms. Thus the people who staff these organisations tend to be either high Normals or Hustlers who have mimicked the Normal component.
- **Hustlers** are agents. Their ability to tell both sides of a story helps in such fields as stockbroking, merchant banking, real estate, car dealerships and so on. Only individuals with considerable Hustler can handle both buyers and sellers quickly and profitably.
- The **Mover** works best in service industries which deal with numbers of people, such as retailing and fast foods. The enthusiasm and energy of Movers make them excellent employees and later managers in these industries.

- **Doublecheckers** are preoccupied with security. Suitable industries include those concerned with potential disasters, such as insurance or transport monopolies.
- **Artists** are creative, iconoclastic yet withdrawn. They are found in industries where creativity is critical to success such as advertising and fashion.
- **Politician** norms of behaviour tend to be followed in bureaucracies and big companies. Position, office size and status symbols are some manifestations of this component. It is also common in the largest company within an industry.
- **Engineers** tend to dominate building design companies and consultants, where the work flow tends to be a succession of projects. To succeed in an Engineering organisation you have to be successful at planning and completing projects.

If you are unsure about the norms of a company, look at its annual report. It is unnecessary to look inside or calculate any financial ratios, just examine the cover. If it is bright and flashy it is probably a Hustler organisation. If it contains many photographs of people it probably has a Mover culture. A subtle and creative touch suggests an Artist company. Pictures of successfully completed projects suggest an Engineer organisation.

Position

Just as organisations may have dominant components, so too do certain positions or functions.

Successful General Managers, who need logic, ceaseless energy and a thirst for success, tend to be a combination of Normal, Mover and Politician. Marketing people generally succeed if they are emotional and have lots of enthusiasm and a manipulative streak. Thus marketing personnel tend to be low in Normal, and high in Mover and Hustler. Administrative staff requires the ability to double-check and do monotonous and detailed work, and so tend to combine strong Normal and Doublechecker components. Personnel managers need to be able to meet a number of people during the day for interviews and other meetings so generally have high Mover component. On the other hand they need to be sensitive so need high Artist. IT managers generally come from software backgrounds which tend to hire people with a lot of Doublechecker (to check the code) and Engineer (to complete the project). To rise above the ruck the individual needs a lot of Politician as well. Besides the position in an organisation, another useful clue is a manager's personal assistant. Since like attracts like, managers often select staff who have similar components to their own.

Thus, the organisation that an individual works for and his position within that organisation can be important clues to the personality. While you will frequently get square pegs in round holes, generally you do find that managers work for organisations and in positions that suit their personality best.

Dress

Dress is another very important clue as to the dominant personality components. The fashion industry bases its appeal on the assumption that clothes and appearance are a reflection of the personality: *The apparel oft proclaims the man*, or, the modern equivalent, *I dress to make a statement about myself.*

Normals tend to wear high quality, conservative clothes in sober colours such as grey. Men's ties tend to be conservative and often show some form of repetitive emblem representing a club, school or university.

Dress is a key clue for the Hustler component. The clothes are generally glitzy, if not flashy. For example, a male Hustler generally wears red or orange striped ties. Both the male and female Hustler often wear ostentatious watches and bracelets. The female Hustler will typically have gold rings on at least two or three fingers and heavy gold earrings. When they wear casual clothes, they are often open-necked showing off gold chains and necklaces. Another clue is that Hustlers often wear designer label clothes, as they love to drop names.

Movers and Engineers tend to have a tousled appearance. Movers usually have their coats off, collar unbuttoned and sleeves rolled up. They often appear to be rushing from one task to another. They like to wear casual clothes such as jeans, running shoes and loose fitting shirts and pullovers. Movers like bright colours and patterns. They often have a message on their clothes such as *Don't Worry—Be Happy*, either in the form of a button, or as a slogan on a T-shirt.

Engineers get very wound up in their work and are disinterested in dress. So their shirts slip out of their trousers and their ties will slip without being noticed. The model Engineer is the absent-minded professor who puts on an unmatched pair of socks. Engineers are interested in technology and often are the first to own the latest technical advance such as G3 mobile phone, Bluetooth earpiece or PDA (Personal Digital Assistant). They typically have a row of pens in their shirt pocket or a Swiss knife on a belt. Female Engineers often have something useful hanging around their neck such as a fob watch or a ballpoint pen. Both sexes often wear striped shirts, which are in non-classic colours or patterns.

Doublecheckers tend to choose good quality clothes as they believe cheap clothes are poor acquisitions because they will soon fall apart. As the Doublechecker male has an overpowering need for security he too wears club ties. He usually has a short back-and-sides haircut. There is a Mother Earth colouring about Doublecheckers' clothes; browns and greens tend to dominate. Doublechecker women tend to have big handbags filled with all sorts of make-up and other items as a precaution against any unforeseen eventuality.

Artists tend to wear very imaginative clothes and be in the forefront of fashion. The ties of the men and the dress of the women often contain unusual patterns. Sometimes they choose clothes that are odd-ball. Another common dress code for the Artist is totally black.

As noted earlier Politicians often wear navy and are conservative in nature. However they are very keen on uniforms. They like working in organisations that have uniforms and designing new ones.

Office

If you meet people either in their home or office you then have another excellent clue as to their dominant components. While the Politician's mode of dressing tends to be conventional and nondescript, it is the offices of the Politicians that give them away. It is often in the most dominant position in the building and larger than the surrounding offices. Even if the offices are the same size the Politician's office contains status symbols such as nameplates, degrees and certificates on the walls. Politicians generally place their desks in a dominant position. Both Politicians and Hustlers try to have entertaining areas if it is at all possible.

By contrast, the office of the Artist sometimes has the desk facing away from a view or window. The office furniture and lighting is typically of a modern, creative design. The desk is sometimes untidy as the Artist detaches himself from reality. Some form of original creativity often hangs on the wall.

The Hustler, on the other hand, often has a flashy reproduction on the wall and flamboyant decor. Because they are usually divorced you will often see a family picture with the ex-wife missing.

Doublecheckers tend to have pictures of their family in a prominent position on their desk but in this case all the family is in the photograph. They cram their offices with files as they cannot bear to throw anything away and they have to keep a copy of everything—just in case.

Engineers often have timetables, project charts and pictures of big projects such as bridges, buildings or aeroplanes hanging on the wall. They usually have shelving crammed with books on a number of diverse topics. Their desks are usually untidy but they tend to know where everything is to be found.

Movers also have untidy desks cluttered with the working papers of several simultaneous projects. Because they see things in black and white they often have slogans on the wall.

Normals are usually neat and tidy in their work and so have neat and tidy desks, situated in a neat and tidy office. If they have a bookcase it is often filled with old leather books. Another clue to the Normal is the paintings they hang on the wall. Typically they are landscapes although sometimes you may even see a painting of a founder.

Gambit

Gambit is a term taken from the game of chess and refers to the opening moves made by a player. Using the same metaphor you can work out what drives a person by their own opening moves. Did he or she keep you waiting and when you do meet do they address you informally or formally? The Gambit is an important clue to your prospect's personality. First, is the prospect punctual? If they are punctual then it is a safe bet that you are dealing with one of the following:

- a Normal who is on time because that is the socially correct thing to do,
- a Hustler because winners are on time and losers are late,
- an Artist because they are sensitive about other people's feelings and do not like to keep them waiting, or
- an Engineer, because time is money to an Engineer.

> "The six clues of *talk*, *organisation*, *position*, *dress*, *office*, and *gambit* form a mnemonic, TOPDOG."

If, on the other hand, you are kept waiting, you are dealing either with a Mover, because they have become distracted on their way to the appointment, or a Politician, who keeps you waiting to show you who is the more important.

You then distinguish between those who keep you waiting and those who do not by how they address you. Normals will address you formally and will not use first names until well into the meeting. Hustlers are friendly and genial and while they're on time, they generally will address you informally rapidly moving to first names. Artists (who are also punctual) will, because they take quite some time to get to know people, address you formally while Engineers do the opposite—they tend to be reasonably friendly and will address you informally. Of those that will keep you waiting Movers will immediately apologise, immediately get on first name terms and their warm enthusiastic smile will immediately put you on their side and make you forget their tardiness. Politicians on the other hand, will not apologise for keeping you waiting, and will be formal and fairly aggressive in their first few moments.

The six clues of *talk, organisation, position, dress, office,* and *gambit* form a mnemonic, TOPDOG. (The word, mnemonic, is derived from the name of the Greek goddess of memory and is defined as something that helps the memory. The technique is to form an acronym from the first letters of the words of the various steps. RADAR, for example, stands for Radio Detecting And Ranging.)

TOPDOG is a very useful way of remembering how to analyse people. After a meeting, immediately go through the six clues. If you are preparing for a meeting, you can carry out some analysis of the organisation beforehand. If you know the person's position, you have another possible clue about their personality. While you're waiting for the meeting, the punctuality of the person is another clue. You will have the opportunity to do further analysis when you walk into the person's office, examine their dress and listening to the way they talk. Remember, what you're trying to do is establish one or two key dominant components and then from that analysis adjust your management style accordingly.

Step 4: Relationship Management

Emotional Intelligence professionals regard relationship management as perhaps the most important of the four EQ skills. We now have a very useful model for the manager to use handling relationships with peers and sub-ordinates. This chapter tells you how to do this for each of the seven components. Each component is discussed in four sections. First we describe the working environments each component prefers; then we give some tips about training each component. The next section gives some advice on how to deal with a stereotype who is frustrated at work and whom you may need to criticise, and the final section is some suggestions about how to gain co-operation.

> **"Emotional Intelligence professionals regard relationship management as perhaps the most important of the four EQ skills."**

The Normal

The first stereotype we shall deal with is the Normal. Now remember, the Normal is driven by the desire for order and is characterised as a conservative, self-disciplined, inhibited individual who follows social norms.

Normals like neat and tidy work environments and make excellent administrators and analysts. They perform well in jobs that require a logical, orderly approach.

They generally need only standard initial training and instructions. When giving instruction you should be objective, clear, and logical.

Normals generally cause little difficulty to superiors and fellow workers and work well in most organisations because they have good self-control and follow procedures and group norms. They rarely show signs of dissatisfaction and make the best of whatever circumstances they find themselves in. Normals may need to have some guidance to help them relax their inhibitions, particularly in high-pressure temporary project team situations where the need for warm relations and a sense of humour is necessary.

When praising a Normal, particularly emphasise their constructive approach to their work. Congratulate them on any achievements made during the past year or any programmes of training or self-improvement they have started or completed. If they have a good reputation among their co-workers, tell them about it, as they regard that as most important.

If you have to criticise them, frame it as a constructive suggestion towards their self-improvement. Try to act as a constructive friend concerned with trying to help them improve. Discuss the suggestions specifically and try to show how their present actions are inconsistent with self-improvement. Finally be mild and objective in any criticism—most important of all, avoid emotion.

Remember that for the Normal the world is black and white and they apply the rules, regardless of the circumstances. There are some jobs where being a stickler for rules is an advantage. On the other hand you may find yourself suggesting that more flexibility might improve efficiency (which is a magic word to a Normal).

Remember if the Normal is not intelligent they can cost a company a lot of money because of bad decisions. Normals will go to court over an issue because they absolutely know they are in the right, even though all the legal advice is to settle. A good approach is to try and understand their point of view and respectfully disagree.

When seeking to secure their cooperation, be objective and unemotional when describing a new proposal and emphasise the constructive aspects. Indicate any opportunities for self-improvement and show how the idea will result in better working methods. Use logic and references. Normals also prefer logic to emotion and are uncomfortable with emotional presentations.

Normals want to feel part of a group and a good approach is to use references or expert reports, especially from organisations and people with whom the individual would be familiar. A good technique is to refer to a previous decision or situation. In this way you generate an internal reference that is both known and credible.

The Hustler

The Hustler requires a completely different management approach. As we said earlier, the Hustler is dominated by the desire for material success. They are self-interested, shrewd and astute.

They make good salespeople and seek work in environments that provide rapid rewards. Hustlers want the best possible working conditions and will be unhappy if their work place, car, or other corporate benefits are below the average standard for the organisation.

When training a Hustler as a new employee, take a direct approach and tell them they must do it your way. Warn them against taking short-cuts; Hustlers tend to twist the job to suit themselves.

Congratulate Hustlers on their good showing. Tell them how senior management have noticed their performance and mentioned it to you. Praise them personally and directly—do not worry about overdoing praise, they can take it. If they have any trappings because of their personal success (for example a new car or a new suit) mention it, praise their taste and say how you are sure more is bound to come.

If you have to criticise them, tell them frankly and specifically what they must do. If you see or hear of a Hustler doing something wrong, do not ignore it. Pick them up immediately. Otherwise you will find your silence is taken as condoning their actions, and then if you do subsequently criticise them you will find you will be accused of inconsistency. You need to be strict with Hustlers; they respect it. If they don't think you are wise to them they will think you are soft and manipulate you for their own advantage.

If you are going to criticise them be prepared for excuses. You need to be sure of your facts, and remain calm as they blame other people. Tell them what the proper procedure is and penalise them accordingly. Indicate how their breaking the rules was foolhardy, and point out what they stand to lose in the future if they continue to do so.

If a Hustler is intelligent they will be charming and can talk their way out of most confrontations. They will also be successful although it may be due to a lack of ethics or mistreatment of colleagues, whom they use to further their own ends. Terminating a Hustler is difficult because they are the types who are more inclined to go into battle and bring unfair dismissal. If you are managing a Hustler manager you must make sure you put very strict barriers around them to minimise damage they may do. Another approach is to either do an interstate or inter-country transfer or persuade a competitor to poach them.

Remember frustrated Hustlers are a problem in the workplace. They may show childish selfishness and feign ill-health, or they may seek special favours for personal reasons. They may push work onto others and slow down their own output. They will be outspoken about money, complaining they are not paid enough and try to generate ways of increasing their take-home pay.

For new proposals stress immediate gains, as they are particularly responsive to these. Talk freely about any financial rewards (or the threat of financial loss). Hustlers like and believe they understand money. On the other hand, as Hustlers only see the short-term, stress any long-term financial benefits because they tend to miss them. Because Hustlers are social climbers do not hesitate to mention any opportunities for working with high-flyers or showing how the proposal may benefit their image.

When describing the benefits of your project stress any immediate and personal gains. If introducing the project helps make the Hustler more visible in the organisation and will therefore help his or her image, say so. The Hustler is a vain creature and appeals to the ego work wonders. Another technique is to show how the project will help the Hustler move up into higher social groups. The Hustler is a potential socialite and will embrace such suggestions with relish. Of all the components, Hustlers are the only types you should wine and dine, particularly at the latest fashionable restaurants.

The Mover

Movers are active, social, enthusiastic individuals who need to work in jobs where there is a lot of people contact, like sales and customer service. If they are to do detailed work they must be removed from distractions. Movers may need fairly close supervision to ensure they do not spend excessive time in social chatter and that they stick to the job at hand. They like to do lots of things at once, but unfortunately often finish nothing. You should also be careful of entrusting Movers with confidential information because of their tendency to gossip.

When training a Mover as a new employee, take a friendly but businesslike approach. Movers love to talk and can side-track you from a training program. Remember to keep to the point. You need to present material in some detail and continually check to make sure they understand. Movers are inclined to race ahead believing they understand when they have not really grasped the key points about an issue or program.

Praise a Mover by saying that they are good team players and explain how other members of the organisation like them for their good nature, friendliness and approachability. When talking to them, be direct, emotional and personal, as Movers dislike cold fish.

If you need to criticise a Mover, be friendly but serious. Do not let a Mover joke you off the track. If you need to criticise them do it immediately—too much happens to them in the interim if you delay. Be direct in any criticism and distinguish carefully between your attitudes to them as a person and their actions. Be prepared for an emotional outburst—just remain calm—and then continue after it is expended.

When frustrated, Movers find it very difficult to concentrate. They become restless, stopping work frequently and seeking people to talk to. They end up talking for the sake of talking. Movers may have sudden outbursts of temper that they soon forget but everyone else remembers.

To commit a Mover to a new proposal begin by describing the concept in a friendly, enthusiastic, emotional manner. Just remember to 'Smile—Smile—Smile'. If you are enthusiastic, the Mover will respond with even more enthusiasm. In complete contrast to selling to a Normal you should forget logic and use as much emotion as possible. It is also important to remember that the Mover is easily distracted and finds it difficult to concentrate. You should therefore disregard details, as the Mover prefers to deal with general concepts. Make sure they listen and keep them to the point. Movers may get carried away with the proposal and lose the original concept. Do not use any more details than is necessary. Movers are easily bored.

As the Mover is full of energy and sociability, you should stress the group benefits of your proposal. Another good technique with Movers is to slowly go through your organisation chart establishing benefits for as many departments as possible.

If the proposal requires a project team, introduce the Movers to as many members as possible. The Mover is happiest visiting outside offices and inspecting reference sites. If you can engender a feeling of teamwork then you will maximise the likelihood of acceptance. Once you have established some key benefits, keep repeating them. Movers are so easily distracted that they soon forget the benefits of your proposal and you as well. Keep beaming back and you will usually get a warm reception from the Mover. If you fail to gain approval, keep contacting the Mover every day. Unlike Normals and Hustlers who would find such behaviour irritating, Movers like to meet people. Engage in some social conversation, tell a joke, and then repeat the benefits of your proposal.

The Doublechecker

We now know that Doublecheckers are driven by their desire for security and their need to avoid risk; consequently they usually have stable job histories.

However, they often express dissatisfaction because of their tendency to see the faults in any situation. Thus, even though they are loyal employees they sometimes develop a reputation as complainers. You need not worry about their complaints; just give them the same conditions as other people. You do need to remember that they are hypochondriacs—they are inclined to seek sympathy and will consider those who do not give it as unfeeling. Consequently, as their manager, you have to spend some time each day expressing sympathy and asking about the family.

Doublecheckers make good administrators particularly in roles that require double checking such as payroll or auditing. They are compassionate, sympathetic people so they generally work well in repetitive customer service situations that do not need innovative solutions to problems.

Make sure you set Doublechecker employees workloads that they can handle. If they think the load is excessive, they will deem the task impossible to do, and do nothing except complain about how unfair the management is. The secret is to set a reasonable workload, complete with a time schedule for separate tasks in order to provide some moderate pressure. If you keep Doublecheckers busy then they will not have enough time either to complain or worry. Always remember Doublecheckers suffer from an extreme lack of confidence, so that if something goes wrong, they immediately blame themselves for the failure.

When training Doublecheckers, go slowly and patiently. Make sure that they are following. Doublecheckers tend to become preoccupied with a specific point and to miss others—do not try to tell them everything at once. A good trick is to work through the initial steps with them to get them started. Remember Doublecheckers find it difficult to start new tasks.

You cannot praise a Doublechecker just once a year during a performance appraisal. You need to do it frequently to boost their confidence, which will in turn increase their energy output. When they complete a task, compliment them freely and do it directly and personally. If they are stuck, remind them of their past successes. Commend their natural caution if it is appropriate.

If you have to criticise a Doublechecker for a mistake, remember they will feel badly about it anyway so use some restraint. Make sure you distinguish between the person and the behaviour. If you criticise a Doublechecker personally you may end up destroying their confidence. A better technique is to ask them to be critical of their actions and jointly try to develop suggestions for future constructive actions. Finally, after criticising a Doublechecker, encourage them and assure them that you know they can do the job properly.

It is difficult to convince Doublecheckers about new proposals. Getting agreement from a Doublechecker takes a long time. A good technique is to ask for their criticism of present activities and use their answers to lead to constructive suggestions. Refer to past successes if that is possible. Because they are so cautious and prone to double-checking they will usually have been successful in implementing a previous proposal. Do not hurry your outline. Doublecheckers are not alert and are slow on the uptake. Go slowly so they understand your proposal and gain confidence in it. Remember that they will regard any new proposal pessimistically. Therefore you must be prepared to counteract their gloom with optimism and assume that the proposal is going ahead.

The Artist

Artists, as we have established, are individualistic. They prefer to work alone but can work well in small groups where they have established intensive relationships such as in the creative team of an advertising agency, or a group of researchers. Remember that Artists do have strong egos and set themselves high standards. They are able to work well without close supervision. They like to be trusted and respond well to delegation.

Make sure when they start a new job or undergo training that you give them the background thinking. Artists work better when they are in the picture. Do not labour detail unnecessarily and encourage them to contribute their own ideas. Artists often do have good ideas but are too shy to mention them.

The secret with Artists is to praise the work and not the person. They see through flattery but accept the implied personal commendation that praising their work will give. If you can mention how the work indicates imagination, insight or tactfulness, do so, for these are qualities that Artists admire. A good technique is to give them a written note of praise expressing confidence in their ability; this avoids personal embarrassment.

If you need to reprimand an Artist do not be personal—criticise the action instead. As their intentions are usually good you do not need to labour the criticism. Artists do not deliberately do the wrong thing, and it is a good idea to ask for their explanation. Then use tact and be constructive in your comments and make sure you do it quietly and briefly. Artists are really apprehensive of people criticising them. They can form hidden resentments and become angry underneath about perceived slights. They may start misplacing files, or forgetting to give you messages and they always have an excuse. Make sure you avoid direct attack because they can be very stubborn, however do document each problem as it arises carefully distinguishing between opinion and fact.

If Artists become frustrated they will use escape mechanisms. A common behaviour is to start sulking. They either withdraw from the workplace at least mentally if not physically, or refuse to deal with people they dislike. Another response is to dodge situations where they feel they may not be accepted. Artists can be passively stubborn and intractable if they feel things are not going their way.

If you need to secure their co-operation over a new proposal see them alone, and spend some time giving them the background to your proposal and the thinking that led up to it. You should aim at having several short person-to-person meetings rather than one long heavy presentation. Begin any presentation by giving a history of the project. Go into some detail and throughout the story ask them to imagine what was happening. Appealing to their imagination and asking for suggestions are good techniques with the Artist. Once they understand your proposal Artists will often come up with useful ideas. If they do suggest an impractical idea treat it gently, show respect for it, and explain why it will not work. If involved in a group discussion, avoid bringing them into too great a prominence. A great technique is to jointly work out a proposal on a white board where you interact side-to-side rather than face-to-face.

Use visual words. Among some of the more useful visual words are:

Clear	Have I been clear on how this proposal will work?
Examine	Let's examine how the company will do this.
Focus	Focus in on this idea; you will see how the company will benefit.
Imagine	Imagine how your staff will like this.
Look	Look at the quality of this report.
Picture	Have you got a picture in your mind about how this will work?
View	How do you imagine our board will view this proposal?

The Politician

Politicians seek power and prestige over other people. They like jobs that give them importance and where they will be noticed. Politicians particularly like signs of status such as nameplates, titles, assigned parking places, and the like. If left unsupervised, Politicians will go their own way. A good technique is to carry out unannounced spot checks to keep them on track. When dealing with Politicians it is important to be firm but unemotional. Also make sure they listen.

Politicians hate to admit ignorance so when training make it easy for them. Do not ask embarrassing questions, nor should you show off your own knowledge. If they do suggest something show respect for it.

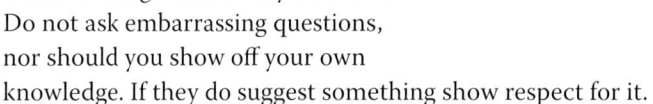

Praise Politicians for their sound judgement, decisiveness or drive. Politicians pride themselves on having these qualities. It is a good technique to praise their standing compared to others. Use the performance appraisal time to boost them personally and directly. They like that.

If you have to criticise a Politician first make absolutely sure of your facts and present them firmly. Do not be hesitant or doubtful; Politicians can sense any weakness in your case and will capitalise on it. Do not accept any excuses or alibis. On the other hand, allow them a face-saver if it can be done factually. You do not need to wait for a formal performance appraisal to criticise a Politician. Their natural suspicion means they quickly pick up hints and subtle suggestions about a need for a change in behaviour.

Politicians are naturally suspicious and more self-protective than most employees. If they become frustrated, Politicians can become quite outspoken and critical of either the organisation they work for or management. If they make a mistake they will project the blame onto someone else or rationalise the mistake. If they believe that they have been treated unfairly, they can spend considerable time seeking revenge. This can severely affect the quality and quantity of their work.

A good way of gaining their support for a new proposal is to ask them for their help and tell them you value their opinions. Politicians respond well to flattery. Their egos make them unable to stop themselves from helping you. Another technique is to find out where both your opinions concur and then widen the area of common agreement. However, do not let them express dogmatic opinions too early because they will not retract them. The Politician, as the complementary component to the Artist, can be equally stubborn and will often refuse to change an opinion once it is given. Thus, if you are trying to get a Politician to change suppliers, you should never first ask the Politician if the company is happy with its present supplier. Instead you should ask indirect questions. Instead of, 'How many times has our courier service been late?' ask, 'In your opinion, what are the criteria that should be used in choosing a courier service?' Politicians love to answer indirect questions (unlike the Artist) and to give opinions. The other problem with direct questions is that they may make the Politician seem ignorant; this is disastrous and nothing will more quickly create antagonism. Politicians are reluctant to change their opinions, no matter how forceful or logical the argument. This is in contrast to the Doublechecker who, if you ask if the company is satisfied with a present supplier, will dredge up small incidents of dispute that happened five years ago.

The technique with the Politician is to sow the seeds and let them germinate. The best method is to use examples of large organisations as references. Another technique is to quote from articles in well-known magazines. For the Politician, 'big is best'. If you can, try to establish the idea that adopting the proposal will draw favourable attention to the Politician. For instance, if a proposal has to go to the Board, use the Politician's name on the front page of the proposal and, if possible, sprinkle it throughout the document. Another method is to show how the proposal will make the Politician (and the company) the leaders in their country, if not the world.

As the Politician is opinionated and dogmatic you are bound to have differences. Politicians like people who stand up to them—it proves that they share with the Politician the key characteristic of backbone, so you must stand up to the Politician when needed, but you should be tactful and avoid putting the Politician on the defensive.

Use auditory words with a Politician. Among the more useful are:

Hear	Do you hear what I am saying?
Listen	Listen carefully. This next part of our conversation is important.
Quiet	We describe our service people as the quiet achievers.
Amplifies	This reference report from one of the Top 20 companies amplifies what I have been telling you.
Sound	How does this proposal sound to you so far?
Tell	Doesn't the quality of this proposal tell you something?
Talk	Have you heard anyone talk about this project before?

If you do have an argument with a Politician and it begins to get heated, suggest that you leave and come back later. This 'another meeting' technique works well and will usually defuse the crisis. Politicians have arguments all the time. They soon forget any argument once it has been resolved and finish by referring to it as a minor disagreement. It is unresolved conflicts that lead to a grudge. Politicians, although trying, are decision-makers. If you appeal to their need for status and prestige and use auditory words you should obtain favourable results.

The Engineer

Engineers prefer to work in organisations where they can devote themselves to their tasks without interruption. Engineers are useful employees in that they derive satisfaction from completing jobs that others would find monotonous.

Engineers have good attention to detail and will work conscientiously on projects without supervision. If you do not want them to pay meticulous attention to detail, tell them how far you want them to go. For example, if you want a three-page summary say so, or else you could well receive a 40-page analysis.

When teaching an Engineer about new jobs do it in a logical sequence, step-by-step. Take it reasonably slowly, covering the topic in some detail.

Engineers consider that they have a detached, objective attitude to their work even though of all components they are probably the most obsessive about it. This is a good attitude to praise. Engineers are generally fixated about quality. Consequently it is a good idea to reinforce this fixation by mentioning that you will continue to have confidence in their ability to meet quality standards. You should also praise their thorough attention to detail and their steadfast ambition.

If you need to criticise an Engineer do so in a direct, matter-of-fact, unemotional way. Discuss any shortcomings of their work in detail. You will need to make sure you have their attention and they are not concentrating on some other project. A good approach is to emphasise the need to attend to overall responsibilities as well as details.

If Engineers become frustrated they typically show one of two reactions. They either start spending an obsessive amount of time on detail or they become increasingly irritable without apparent reason. Occasionally they may have a sudden emotional outburst out of all proportion to the obvious cause.

Gaining the support of an Engineer for a new proposal is relatively easy. First advise them ahead of time (whenever possible) because Engineers need time to adjust themselves and marshal their thoughts. Make sure you arrange to consult them when they are free, as Engineers hate to be abruptly interrupted. Appeal to their need to complete worthwhile projects, then outline the proposal in some detail and continue to stress the overall objective. You will probably need to proceed slowly, for Engineers tend to be left behind in their exhaustive consideration of earlier points. Finally make sure your proposal is completely set out to show an organised plan with the important details. Engineers appreciate thoroughness.

You need to remember that the Engineer is probably already working on another inspired project. So your first task is to work out the current timetable of projects and put the introduction of your project at the top of the list of new projects. This is most easily done by asking about the Engineer's present list of projects and establishing when the one they are currently working on will be finished. Suggest that when this project finishes the logical step would be to spend two or three days establishing priorities. You should then try to make an appointment at that time. Do not make the appointment for an earlier date—the Engineer finishes projects on time. When approaching the Engineer, make sure you have an appointment (remember, Engineers become irritated if interrupted or distracted from their current task). Throughout the presentation stress the dominant benefit of your project and how useful it is.

You will have to go into detail—the Engineer is the technical buyer. You should try to provide as much detail as possible in the form of brochures or manuals. I once supplied to a prospect every technical manual on one computer range that I could before I got the sale. It needed six visits of ten minutes each. Every meeting was the same; I would first collect the three 200-page manuals that I left behind at the last meeting, try to answer one or two questions and then hand over another three manuals. My only worry was that the computer would be obsolete before the prospect had completed all his reading. Engineers are bookworms and you should flood them with information about your product.

When presenting to the Engineer go slowly and word your proposal in terms of a 'plan', 'task' or 'project'. Engineers prefer thoroughness and attention to detail. They can be exhaustive in their questions so you should prepare for long meetings.

Use action-feeling words during presentations.
Good examples of such words are:

Feel	How do you think management will feel about it?
Grasp	Have you grasped the concept behind the proposal?
Handle	How do you currently handle this problem?
Hold	Hold everything—the answer has slipped my mind.
Respond	How will the board respond to this proposal?
Stress	I must stress how useful this project will be to our company.
Touch	Touch this prototype and get a feel for how it will work.
Hot, cold or lukewarm	Are you hot, cold or lukewarm about the proposal?

Engineers prefer to handle or touch a product, so a trial run or demonstration in which they use the product themselves is generally a good way of convincing them of the merits of a proposal. If you cannot organise a hands-on demonstration or a prototype trial then, as a last resort, use other customers as references and describe how they used or responded to the product.

Building Teams

A common management task is to create a new team. This can be for the launch of a new product or the opening of a new branch. Sometimes an outside manager is appointed as a replacement with the instructions to re-invigorate the current team or effect a turnaround. This is often a new manager's first true test.

Of course in such a situation there are a number of management techniques that have stood the test of time such as setting goals and objectives, defining responsibilities, providing regular feedback, weekly team meetings and quarterly reviews.

However the Humm can play a very useful role in team building, particularly in overcoming two of the biggest mistakes a new manager can make.

We like those best who are like ourselves.

The old saying that opposites attract may be true in the realm of physics but does not hold in human relations. A study by Klohnen and Luo looked at the profiles of 291 newlyweds who had participated in the Iowa Marital Assessment Project. The results showed that couples had highly similar attitudes and values. Moreover, once people were in a committed relationship, it was primarily personality similarity that influenced marital strength and happiness, and personality differences that led to more friction and conflict in daily life.

This is a red flag to a manager with regard to potential hirings. Instead of selecting the best person for a job, we end up choosing someone who has a similar personality to ourselves.

A better approach is to use the Humm and try to define what sort of personality would best do a new job. Then armed with that knowledge, recruit the most appropriate candidate.

Make sure your team contains a diverse set of personalities.

If you do set about ensuring your team contains a diverse set of personalities then it can suffer from accelerated 'Groupthink'. Groupthink is defined where groups agree to pursue goals with which the individual members do not agree. If the members of the group all have similar personalities then this process can be accelerated. The Bay of Pigs Invasion would be a good example of this. The decision to execute this disastrous military campaign was made with almost unanimous agreement by President John F. Kennedy and his advisors. These advisors were, almost without exception, very similar in background and personality to the President and lacked military command experience. General David M. Shoup, Commandant of the Marine Corps at the time and not part of the group, predicted failure for the invasion, which went forward with disastrous results.

Richard LeBlanc, a Canadian business management professor, studied some 40 Boards over a period of five years. He concluded that key to a successful board was to have a diverse set of personality types including Change-Agents, Consensus-Builders, Counsellors and Challengers.

> **Instead of selecting the best person for a job, we end up choosing someone who has a similar personality to ourselves.**

I particularly remember the first day I learnt about the Humm technique. Kevin Chandler, who was giving the course, described how they had conducted psychological profiles on the ten members of the executive management team of what was at that time Australia's leading property developer. He went to see the Managing Director, who was a huge MP, with the results. The MD started the meeting by saying that he was sure the tests demonstrated that his company had one of the best management teams in Australia. Kevin replied in the negative, saying that too many of the team were MPs like himself, and in an industry notoriously cyclical like building, it was critical that one or two members of the team had a lot of D component. Unfortunately in this management team, nobody had high D, so the company was particularly vulnerable. The Managing Director, optimistic and forthright, dismissed the report as psychobabble. Within 12 months the company had collapsed and at the time was Australia's biggest corporate failure.

This was a lesson I never forgot and as I moved up the management ladder, I always tried to make sure that as a number two I had reporting to me someone who would compensate for my weaker personality components. My D is low and this means I have a high tolerance for risk. This proved to be very successful as it would give me a different perspective on many decisions and often prevented me making serious mistakes.

Management Styles

There is no conclusive evidence that any one managerial style is the best. It appears that a successful managerial style depends on the task, the nature of the subordinates and surrounding conditions. The choice of style thus depends in major part on the manager's personality and those of his or her subordinates.

Lower level leaders and managers have to be task-oriented and technically competent, but can get by with a lesser level of people skill. However, as a general rule, the higher the level in an organisation, the more important it is for managers to be competent in interpersonal relations. As one moves higher, task competency becomes less important. At higher management levels people skills become critical.

Another critical issue in management is how much decision-making power a leader should share with subordinates. Typically managerial styles have been placed in a continuum from autocratic through consultative to delegating. Autocrats are most successful in a task-oriented position where the manager would assign tasks to group members, emphasise the meeting of deadlines, expect workers to follow routines, stress being ahead of the competition, let group members know what was expected of them, and so forth. Democrats are most successful in participative organisations. Then the manager needs to be friendly and approachable, and help subordinates with personal problems, listen to group members, and stand up for subordinates.

Consequently a model of human behaviour is most important for the professional manager. The previous section demonstrated how the Humm is an important tool for mangers to use in the selection, management, and motivation of subordinates. In this section we will analyse how the different components affect both our management styles and our decision-making.

The Normal

Normals are perfectionists who follow the rulebook. They begin meetings with agendas and finish with action plans. They are calm under pressure, and often appear as textbook managers. Unfortunately some people do not like working for Normals because they are perceived as cold, colourless and lacking a good sense of humour.

Normals are generally conservative. They will be rational in their decision-making. Because of their perfectionist tendencies, Normals will often conclude that they cannot make a decision now because they do not have sufficient information. Normal managers will often prefer to call in a consultant or outside expert, and you need to ensure that the cost of achieving a decision does not outweigh the benefits.

The Hustler

Hustlers are commercial realists. They tend to be very cost conscious except for their own rewards which can be excessive. Hustlers think of themselves first, then their team, and then the organisation. They justify this attitude by saying all managers think the same. People often work well for Hustlers initially because of this feeling that they are dedicated to the team but then become unhappy working for them because Hustlers are insensitive to the social effects of their actions.

Hustlers will evade responsibility by shifting the blame to others. Hustlers may skirt the edge of the law and will try and work company procedures in their favour. If they have low Normal they may be dishonest if they think they can get away with it. Hustlers lack a conscience and are inclined to disregard the interest and welfare of others. On the other hand if given a task of cost cutting or retrenchment, they can achieve it fairly quickly and ruthlessly.

Hustlers are opportunistic. They like the excitement of gambling and will take risks for quick gains. They will often sacrifice the long-term for the short-term. They will also approach decisions from a personal standpoint. Hustlers will look at a proposal with the attitude of, 'What's in it for me' and react accordingly.

The Mover

Movers can make good team managers because of their cheerful enthusiasm. People like working for them because they have a natural interest in people and they spread their energy through the team. They have a good sense of humour and are generally alert and responsive to changes in the environment.

Unfortunately Movers do have weaknesses in their managerial style. They rely too much on intuition and often act before they think. They often accomplish little despite great activity. They may have an initial enthusiasm for projects but often fail to follow through.

Movers tend to have strong emotional likes and dislikes that may lead to impulsive decision-making. They tend to be influenced more by the person presenting a proposal than the proposal itself.

The Doublechecker

Doublecheckers like working for Doublechecker managers because they perceive them as compassionate caring people. Doublecheckers are best as managers either in administration or maintenance situations where it is important that nothing is missed or forgotten. If the task requires speed, enthusiasm or innovation then the Doublechecker will generally not be up to it.

Thus they should not work in sales or marketing, but in finance or administration where risk avoidance is a key to success. Doublecheckers can be over-sympathetic to other's misfortunes and will find it very difficult to terminate staff.

Doublecheckers tend to make decisions with reasonable judgement and caution. Their constructive criticism may provide a useful brake to others impetuosity. On the other hand they may spend too much time weighing the facts in order to avoid error. They also tend to worry about trifling issues, and may procrastinate.

The Artist

Artists make good imaginative planners. On the other hand, because they are individualistic they may put their own standards above those of the organisation. For example, in the case that a company expects a certain margin for error in product quality, and builds a warranty provision into the pricing, an Artist manager may demand a zero-defect result from his or her team. Artists can be impractical and detached from reality.

Artists are subtle and indirect and this can lead to confusion when they give instructions. Artists tend to prefer to lead by example rather than driving people by issuing instructions and following up. Artists are not good at meeting new people and making them feel comfortable. Artists are also poor at dismissing employees even if their performance warrants it. They avoid conflict and are easily embarrassed.

Artists are good with abstract decisions that require a lot of planning. They have rich constructive imaginations that can often come up with an innovative solution. Unfortunately they may be too shy to express the solution, or if they do and it is not accepted become passively stubborn until it is. Alternately, if they consider their suggestion may cause harm to other people or departments, they may well refuse to express it because they are very tactful about hurting others.

The Politician

Of all the seven components, the Politician component is the one most likely to be found in a manager. Politicians seek leadership positions and because they are decisive and are able to dominate others they tend to make good managers, provided they have other necessary qualities such as Normal and Mover.

Of course, without other ameliorating components, Politicians will be argumentative and aggressive, and they tend to be domineering and arrogant towards their staff and may even misuse their authority. They are by nature suspicious so often will not co-operate with their fellow managers and so disrupt the operation of an organisation. Staff reporting to Politician managers often consider them to be conceited and boastful. Politicians like to show off their status and brag about their achievements.

Politicians are not afraid of making decisions and once they do will stick to them. The problem with Politicians is that because of their temperament the decision-making process can be too emotional. Politicians love to argue and discuss. They are typically fluent; and can express a case very well in what appears to be a systematic fashion. They know that mastery of the facts is important and will do the work to learn about a subject or at least learn enough to give the appearance of being an expert. Unfortunately, they will often interpret the facts to suit themselves.

Politicians will usually view a decision-making discussion as a contest which they have to win. Frequently they express a view that later they may concede privately to themselves is wrong, but will stubbornly hold to it because to change their mind would be a sign of weakness. Politicians also tend to hold unreasonable grudges and this can bias their judgement.

Their persistence can also cause what is the LBJ effect; called thus after Lyndon Baines Johnson, the 36th President of the United States. Johnson put more resources into the Vietnam War once it became clear it could not be won. High Ps will often escalate an organisation's commitment to a failing course of action. A famous example was the CEO of Montgomery Ward, which was once the leading retailer in the USA. Convinced that the US was going to slide into severe economic depression after World War II, he refused to open any stores until 1957. His competitors did the opposite, opening stores in the new suburbs built in the economic boom and Montgomery Ward slid into oblivion.

Politicians are intimidators. They are willing to use their power to achieve their ends and treat staff reporting to them as expendable resources. They seek to exploit anxieties and weaknesses. Their first meetings with staff are typically confrontational followed by hard and sceptical questioning. I remember one Politician Manager, when going on a first visit to an interstate branch office opening, musing in front of the staff whether he should close the branch. It did not make him popular but for the next six months that branch was the outstanding performer.

> **"Politicians will usually view a decision-making discussion as a contest which they have to win. Frequently they express a view that later they may concede privately to themselves is wrong, but will stubbornly hold to it because to change their mind would be a sign of weakness."**

Politicians use anger well. They are not adverse to causing a commotion nor publicly humiliating staff reporting to them to get attention. Sometimes people make the mistake that the Politician is acting. They are not; anger is a key manifestation of their temperament. They also know that the threat of an angry argument is a deterrent to potential challengers.

Politicians are not transparent. They do not believe in an open, trusting management style. Instead they prefer to keep their staff guessing because they believe it keeps them on their toes. They can also change direction if they need to without losing perceived credibility. If people do not know your intentions or motives, it is easier to catch them by surprise. This, of course, runs counter to the advice of many management text books, and the style can often prove counter-productive. Nevertheless it can be very effective, particularly in large organisations that have become bureaucratic.

The Engineer

If you need to appoint a manager to complete a difficult project such as developing a new product, or implementing a new system, make sure that they have some Engineer component. If Engineers are convinced that the project is worthwhile then they will apply themselves to it with painstaking attention to detail. They will take a systematic and analytical approach to problems and will ensure the task is completed.

While Engineers are good at making sure work is done in an orderly fashion, they are not good with people. They tend to be unemotional and boring conversationalists. Engineers perceive work to be about production and pay little attention to the social issues.

Engineers find it difficult to delegate authority. They can become overly fussy and preoccupied with details. Engineers are methodical decision-makers. They will take a logical, matter of fact approach to a problem. They will often take a decision on their own, when in fact some discussion with other people might have been useful. They can also concentrate too much on details and be quite exhaustive in their analysis of alternatives. Also sometimes, particularly if their Normal is not strong, they can become ecstatic over a project. Then they become impossible to deal with and their decision-making with regard to their pet project may become obsessive and biased.

Combinations

The contribution of each component to the personality depends on its core motivation, the level of Normal, the conflict or harmony with other components, and whether it is overwhelmed by a particularly strong component.

Managers themselves may be classified into two types, operating managers and project managers. Operating managers are the most common and comprise a whole range of managers including general managers, sales managers, administrative managers, production managers, etc. The nature of all these jobs is that while the individual working in the job may change, the job will continue to exist as long as the organisation exists. The essence of the operating manager's role is permanence.

Project managers on the other hand are typically involved in a temporary position. The project manager's job usually has a beginning, middle, and end. The trade-off for this lack of security is job interest and variety.

The mining industry is one that sharply differentiates between these two types of managers. It is said that the person who is good at developing a mine is typically a poor operator of one. Similarly a different type of manager often replaces those who begin businesses (entrepreneurs) once the business reaches a certain size.

Not only are the skills required for these two managerial types different, but some types of temperament are also better suited than others. As a very general rule, successful operating managers will often have some Politician component in their personality, while many successful project managers will have some Engineer component. Hence we have a natural three-way division for combinations of components if we wish to analyse managerial performance:

1. those who contain the Politician (P) component,
2. those who contain the Engineer (E) component,
3. other combinations.

Politician Combinations

Mover-Politician (MP)

MPs have an abundance of driving energy. They have a dynamic, assured attitude, and like all Ps are opinionated and firm in their convictions. They are quick to talk and quick to act. Provided they are channelled in the right direction they can be very effective workers. They like to be at the hub of where things are happening and soon will be organising people to do what they want. They are prepared to argue freely and dispute the ideas of others and are very willing to accept positions of authority. Consequently they have the potential for strong leadership and often become managers.

MPs particularly enjoy jobs that make them look important. Their personalities are fairly powerful and they are inclined to force other people to their way of thinking. Providing they are intelligent and their decisions lead to good results they will be accepted as managers. However if they do not make good decisions or their N component is low then they will be grudgingly accepted and seen as domineering. This antagonism may lead to an MP becoming increasingly arrogant and rash, so that the decision-making in turn becomes even more foolish.

> "They are quick to talk and quick to act. Provided they are channelled in the right direction they can be very effective workers."

The secret to handling an MP is to play up to their sense of superiority. If you want them to do something show how it gives them credit and recognition and emphasise the social and leadership possibilities of the task. MPs like to work in groups, and take decisions so if you can somehow make combine these two factors they will attack the task with their customary energy and decisiveness.

If you need to criticise an MP remember they generally believe that attack is the best form of defence. If they become belligerent, maintain your self-control. Respect their feeling of self-importance and do not put them down. If you can arrive at joint solutions that preserve their concern with personal popularity you will find they accept criticism with equanimity.

Hustler-Politician (HP)

HPs seek power through financial and material gain. They like impressive surroundings and positions of importance. Consequently HPs spend more time than any other combination manoeuvring their way into management positions. The problem with HPs is that if their Normal is low then they may abuse the trust placed in them, and act to satisfy their personal interests alone. They have a strong driving ambition that often leads them to achieve positions of importance. They frequently achieve their goals by charm and flattery. They are quick to accept positions of personal power. They are best in positions that require dictatorial leadership such as managing a money market desk.

HPs can be offhand and ruthless in their treatment of others. Unfortunately they usually take a strong autocratic approach to management and may ride roughshod over their employees. They do not tolerate opposition to their views so today, when a more participative approach is necessary, the management style of the HP may lead to dissent and turnover of staff. If they lack N, subordinates will often fear them.

Another weakness of HPs is that they may sacrifice the long-term for the short-term. They may become so expedient in their decision-making that they lead the organisation to the point of taking unacceptable risks. During the 1980s there were many examples of HP managing directors overextending with debt of the companies for which they had responsibility.

If you need to obtain the co-operation of an HP emphasise the short-term benefits rather than the long-term. A good suggestion is to link the present task with past successes stressing in particular how the result will be to their personal advantage. Moreover, it is useful to appeal to their powerful desire to win in competition. If you can also demonstrate how the project can utilise their aggressiveness, shrewdness and decisiveness you should gain a supporter. HPs like personal and direct praise, of all combinations they both use and react well to flattery.

Hustler-Mover-Politician (HMP)

HMPs want power over people, recognition, and material rewards. They strongly desire respect for their own perceived importance. They are able to work well with people as long as these people are of service to them. They are often 'smooth' talkers and their unlimited drive and verve generally make them very successful business development executives. HMPs are able to produce good accomplishments so long as they think they are getting their own way and their dynamic forcefulness is kept from becoming extreme. Typically their aggressive and energetic personality soon leads to promotion.

HMPs are generally very active in groups and teams, both because they enjoy being with people and regard social activity as a means of furthering their own ends. They are able to show leadership qualities if it suits them, and will take the credit easily for team successes. If faced with personal threat, they will pass the blame readily.

HMPs, particularly if they are working for some form of bonus or commission, can be quite aggressive managers. They often have fixed opinions on how things should operate and when criticised will defend these beliefs fluently and persistently.
If they become frustrated HMPs may become increasingly argumentative, self-defensive and revengeful. They may neglect work and reduce quality and, like HPs, will evade any personal blame.

If you need to gain the help of an HMP try to appeal to their competitive, group spirit. Stress how doing the task will enhance their personal reputation, status and authority over people.

Demonstrate how the project is an opportunity for them to use their abilities and so gain personal rewards. Again flattery appeals to the HMP. You should praise them personally and freely for their aggressiveness, their ability to get things done through people, and their interest in self-advancement. Make sure that you give them full credit for the things they have done well in the past.

Doublechecker-Politician (DP)

The DP suffers from underlying feelings of insecurity but attempts to mask these feelings beneath a veneer of aggressive criticism. They like to look important but will probably never be satisfied. They will be outspoken in criticism of their work situation and will be disgruntled without cause. Often their attitudes have an undertone of bitterness.

Their working arrangements should be the same as for their fellow employees. They need firm, calm, encouraging supervision. As a manager you should emphasise the positive and worthwhile things about their work at all times. They should be given a time schedule for completing their tasks and excuses for failing to complete their tasks should not be accepted.

DPs need to be praised frequently for work well done. You need to encourage them to continue their good performance. Commend them if they make constructive criticisms. Obtaining the co-operation of a DP is difficult. They are negative perfectionists, seeing all those areas in which proposals fall short of ideal. They are outspoken in their criticism of new ideas or innovations. If your proposal is not well thought out, their cynicism will often destroy it. You need to overlook their sarcastic and often unfounded criticism, and counteract their pessimism with optimism. One strategy is to encourage them to see answers rather than problems.

Another technique is to try to show how doing the work well will be to their own advantage and will enhance their reputation. Make sure you stress all the good points of your new proposal—DPs will see all the bad points themselves.

DPs often become either operational or administration managers. They make decisions carefully but having made the decision adhere to it. They suspect that people are trying to take advantage of them and are very watchful for such attempts. Their staff often fear them because they freely criticise shortcomings in their employees' performance.

Artist-Politician (AP)

APs are an unusual combination. The P seeks prestige and status over others, but the A wishes to avoid personal criticism and prefers to work alone. They are defensive lest they be shown up in an unfavourable light. They attempt to hide their personal sensitivity behind a wall of reserve. They like to be trusted on work assignments and resent interference. In essence APs like solitary jobs which make them look important.

Artists are individualistic; APs can be even more so. They tend to take up idealistic causes—often their own peculiar causes. They are extremely stubborn. The manager of an AP employee must ensure that their ideas remain realistic and do not become distorted. Otherwise, because APs will work with great determination in the face of opposition, they will stubbornly refuse to listen to either advice or instructions.

The best way of securing the co-operation of an AP is to appeal both to their imagination and their desires for personal recognition and accomplishments. The best approach is to give the broad orientation of your thinking, then allow them to offer their views, and from their replies widen the area of common agreement. Be clear and carefully distinguish between what are the facts and what are merely your or their opinions.

Deal with APs circumspectly and in one-on-one meetings. You should avoid flattery, otherwise they will become suspicious. Praise their strengths, which are typically their imagination, their ability to visualise new ideas and abstractions and their ability to get work done well.

APs are often promoted to managerial positions in larger organisations. They perform better in staff roles than most people, get noticed at head office and then move into a line position. APs will keep a distance from their staff; indeed AP managers are often regarded by their staff as cold and unresponsive. Given a division that has an entrenched market share, they will often do a very good job, frequently introducing the next strategic innovation in the industry, though it is possible they may get a bee in their bonnet and try to introduce an impractical concept. If they are overruled they may become frustrated and show the behaviour described above. APs may hold a grudge for wrongs they imagine have been done to them.

Engineer Combinations

As noted earlier the Engineer component is frequently found in project managers.

Politician-Engineer (PE)

PEs derive great satisfaction from methodical persistence towards an inspired goal. They prefer to be undisturbed in their efforts to accomplish the objectives they regard as crucial. They become intoxicated with projects that they see as important and as offering them a personal challenge. PEs place stubborn emphasis on the details of an issue. Managers of PEs need to ensure they do not become immersed in detail or unconsciously distort the facts to fit their own preconceived views.

They show great determination in the face of adversity. PEs, if frustrated, may take up a cause and unconsciously distort the facts to prove themselves correct. They can be excessively immersed in unimportant detail and talk at great length about the lack of support they are receiving. They may show extreme irritability about work.

If you need to secure the co-operation of a PE, remember they actively seek recognition of their achievements. Point out the credit and recognition they will be given, particularly if the project is successfully completed, and stress the importance of the activity. If you can, present your concept in terms of a challenging project that contributes to the general aims of the business.

PEs, if a project ties in with their present beliefs and activities, will attack it with ferocity. They will read and learn about it in great detail. They are thorough, persistent and organised when they attack a problem.

As managers, PEs may be very exacting. They are compulsive planners and love to work from checklists. They are systematic and methodical in their work and in their presentations. They expect detailed perfection from other people and from themselves. They can be arrogant about their accomplishments and continuously attempt to impress other people with the importance of their own tasks.

Mover-Engineer (ME)

MEs seek to complete a variety of projects, particularly those that involve people. They prefer to work as a member of a team rather than as an isolated specialist. They do like to work undisturbed at times, particularly when engaged in a challenging project, but at the same time they like people to be near. Supervision of an ME can sometimes be difficult; they may either become lost in the details of a project, or become distracted, depending on which component is stronger at the time. In general, provided the Normal is average to high, they will only need spot-checking, as they work conscientiously at their tasks.

MEs will show enthusiasm for any activity that they think has a purpose. The combination of enthusiastic energy and detailed thoroughness can make them a valuable employee or ally for a new project. If you want to secure their co-operation first outline the goal or objective you wish them to achieve and then urge them to express their ideas. Build on their enthusiasm, show them how it is an opportunity to achieve something worthwhile, and emphasise the human implications of your proposal. Remember that they tend to see other implications of new ideas, so keep to the point and make sure they follow your line of thinking.

MEs, provided they have a reasonable amount of Normal, make popular managers. They are not only concerned with the orderly progress of work but also human issues. They often bring off inspired accomplishments by building up a good team spirit because of their warmth and eagerness. If their Normal is low, however, they are inclined to exhaust themselves physically, and then become over-excitable and irritable. MEs with low N may be unable to determine priorities, scattering their attention among various projects but never finishing them. They will tend to be over-talkative and disorganised in their thinking.

Artist-Engineer (AE)

AEs, as would be expected, are introverts. They do not relate well to people. They prefer to work alone and not be hindered in the performance of a task. They gain satisfaction out of losing themselves in creative projects and completing them successfully. They can produce original ideas, usually on the basis of inspiration. They can visualise abstractions and re-organise details to produce new results. Indeed they have the ideal temperament for pure research. They can be trusted in their work, and, provided they believe their superiors appreciate their efforts and accomplishments, will work well. Supervision should be directed towards keeping their ideals within practical limits. You may need to ensure that their emphasis on details is curbed so that they will be able to meet set time schedules on their tasks.

If you wish to secure the co-operation of an AE, emphasise two things: how worthwhile the project is, and its practical aspects. They like knowing the background to a project and the goal to be achieved. You need only give them the general idea and the details that are not self-explanatory. Make sure you state the degree of thoroughness that the importance of the job merits, or else you may find the AE putting far too much effort into the task.

AEs find it difficult to be managers. They have difficulty in sharing or delegating responsibilities, and strive for idealistic perfection. They are irritated or offended by personal criticism. If their Normal is low they often become preoccupied with useless and impractical detail and are unable to formalise organised plans. AEs exist in their own world and do have difficulty relating to other people.

Hustler-Engineer (HE)

The Hustler-Engineer is another interesting combination. The desire for material success often leads the Hustler to take a short-term perspective, while the Engineer's desire to complete projects makes him take a longer term view of life. This leads to psychological tension.

HEs tend to prefer flashy products with many gadgets and technical points. They often have complicated stereo equipment or sports cars filled with the latest gadgetry and features.

Hustler-Engineers also tend to be erratic about making decisions because they are always wondering whether something better might come along.

Doublechecker-Engineer (DE)

The Doublechecker-Engineer is another difficult individual. Not only will they find fault with a new proposal, they will do so in excruciating detail.
The secret is to let them complain about their present methods as much as possible. If you appeal to their need for change and demonstrate how simple your proposal will be to introduce, DEs, after many tedious meetings, may decide that your project is a promising solution.

To convince a Doublechecker-Engineer you should provide considerable documentation about the technical qualities of your project and a list of happy users.

Other Combinations

Mover-Doublechecker-Artist (MDA)

The MDA is perhaps the most common female combination. MDAs seek friendships through warmth, sympathy, insight and empathy. At work they want to be appreciated as a person, consequently they need friendly and supportive supervision. Give them encouragement and ensure their ideas remain within practical limits. However although they like to be alone part of the time, they also like to have people nearby. As their manager you need to make sure they focus their attention on the task in hand and not idly daydream.

MDAs are sociable, yet contemplative individuals who are prepared to talk about their ideas. Thus if you want to secure their co-operation, appeal first to their imagination. Give them the broad background to the project, and then ask how they would cope with the problem. Remember that they are inclined to worry unnecessarily so you might need to counteract their possible scepticism and hesitancy with optimism. They can visualise abstract ideas and also express them. MDAs are concerned about relationships, so express confidence in their people skills.

MDAs are easily confused so remember to present information in reasonable detail and in a logical sequence. You will probably need to give them constant encouragement when they are learning a new task. Tell them to keep up the good work and remind them of tasks they have already completed.

MDAs if they become managers, find it difficult to make decisions that impact on people. They are cautious decision-makers but fair-minded. They also tend to place harder demands on themselves than on their subordinates.

Hustler-Mover-Doublechecker (HMD)

While MDAs look mainly for security through relationships with people; HMDs look for personal gain or gratification. They are social, talkative effusive people. They are emotional and fun loving. Highly extroverted, they make a good first impression but tend to value friends for the good they can do them. They like impressive surroundings and personal comfort. HMDs need to be closely supervised as they tend to be impulsive and superficial. Make sure they are always reminded that they are dependent on their organisation for their success.

If you need to secure their co-operation stress the immediate gains, particularly if they are social or financial. HMDs are particularly alert to opportunities for financial gain without effort. Appeal to their love of excitement while showing how they can avoid risk to themselves. 'All reward—no risk' is the motto of the HMD. Be direct and to the point because they are essentially realistic thinkers. Do not give them too much detail. It is better to show how they will be able to use their sparkling, animated personality.

HMDs often become managers in sales and service situations, particularly because of their personal charm. At the beginning they are reasonably popular because they are able to show some sympathy and compassion, but that soon goes as their staff begin to take offence at their expedience and superficial attitude. They may attempt to use high pressure tactics on their staff or suppliers but collapse if opposed. They avoid challenging tasks requiring consistent work or application. They are evasive of personal blame and may distort the truth in order to save themselves.

Hustler-Artist (HA)

HAs have the primary aim of pleasing themselves. They give an impression of sincerity that is only skin deep. They do not appear to be openly or obviously self-centred but they are. They will avoid expressing frank opinions and if their Normal is low may be devious in business dealings. They are cunning, wily and circuitous. If their Normal is low they should not be assigned positions of responsibility or authority, as they will merely distort their job to suit themselves. They need firm, even rigid supervision to ensure they adhere to the truth and do not resort to underhand behaviour. They will merely suit themselves unless they are managed tightly and autocratically.

HAs will only respect cunning in other people—you need to demonstrate that you have a shrewd awareness of their attitudes. To secure their co-operation, stress the financial rewards. Appeal to their shrewd imagination and their excellent business acumen. Ask them for their ideas on the solution of problems but do not condone their dishonesty. Warn them about resorting to expedient or cunning behaviour. Make sure that they understand exactly what is required of them and make sure they do not twist facts to suit themselves. Freely acknowledge the past personal successes of the HA, especially where they have shown financial acumen or have struck a good bargain.

HAs, if their Normal is low, can be dangerous managers. They indulge in scheming and plotting to obtain management positions. They devise imaginative fraudulent plans when they occupy such positions. They often change their approach to another unexpected angle, dismaying their subordinates, who become exhausted by the lack of consistency. They are very cynical in their attitudes to people and are always ready to think the worse of others. They will attempt to use their influence and pull strings to advance their own interests and even create trouble for other people if it is expedient. When attacked they will not openly defend themselves but will subsequently lie readily to protect themselves.

Mover-Hustler (MH)

The Mover-Hustler craves excitement and has an active short-term desire for material success. They tend to be friendly yet superficial. If they also have a strong Normal component MHs will use their self-control and to turn their energetic cunning into an aggressive and successful business.

Mover-Artist (MA)

The Mover-Artist is another combination full of tension. The sociability of the Mover strains against the shyness of the Artist. This can lead to paradoxical behaviour with the individual waxing enthusiastic one moment and the next being passively stubborn. MAs must be handled carefully as they may get carried away about a proposal and attribute to it features it does not have. This over-enthusiasm may thus lead to unfortunate repercussions.

Doublechecker-Hustler (DH)

Doublechecker-Hustlers are often suspicious that there is something wrong with a proposal product and that the price is too high. In the same way ferrets hunt out choice rabbits from their burrows, DHs try to ferret out the best deal possible. They take a long time to reach a decision and are always nibbling away for something better. As a manager, do not overreact to their questions and spend too much time with them; instead it is better to answer questions directly and then leave them alone for a few moments to digest the answer.

If you do have an idea that provides value for money, the DH will eventually accept it. They become useful after the purchase, because they are famous among their peers for being careful, fastidious bargain hunters, and become a useful reference.

Doublechecker-Artist (DA)

DAs are conscientious and loyal individuals. They are very careful decision-makers and often ask for advice or support. Under pressure their normally cheerful manner is replaced by obvious feelings of insecurity and they are inclined to 'dither'. When you first meet a DA, he or she can appear shy and diffident and it generally takes them some time be at ease. They dislike people who are aggressive and assertive. DAs show considerable tact, insight, sympathy, empathy and understanding, and as a supervisor this is usually sufficient. However being a nice person does not always work as typically there will be team members who openly take advantage of their easy-going nature.

Gain their support for a proposal using a series of one-on-one meetings and appealing both to their imagination and desire for something better. You will need to go over the first steps carefully. Refer to past successes if that is possible. Give them the background of why you are thinking what you are saying. Tell them repeatedly how confident you are in their ability.

The Glass Ceiling

Is there an emotional difference between men and women? Goleman, in his book *Emotional Intelligence,* cites studies supporting the generalisation that women are more interested in feelings and men in things. Another generalisation he notes is that in relationships, women want to talk about problems while men want to solve them. While generalisations are of some use, the real answer is that we are all individually different including the mix of our core emotions. However, there are some core components that are likely to be stronger in women than in men and vice versa, all other things being equal.

If we refer to a book such as *Men are from Mars, Women are from Venus,* it is possible to draw up a number of emotional characteristics using the John Gray stereotypes. The following table is an attempt to do so with the associated core emotional component against each value.

Female values		Male values	
Communication	M	Power	P
Love	M, D	Achievement/winning	P
Relationships	M, D	Efficiency	E
Beauty	A	Mechanical objects	E
Individualistic dress	A	Uniforms	P
Sharing feelings	D	Competitive sports	P
Talking to one another	M	Solving problems oneself	E
Personal growth	D	Achieving goals	P, E
Intuition	A	Logic	E
Helping and advising others	D	Withdrawing into caves	E

As the table shows high M, D and A components are associated with female values. However, that does not mean a female cannot have high H, P, and E. One who immediately springs to mind is Margaret Thatcher. Her desire to win was amply demonstrated in the way she resentfully stayed in power. Like all high Ps she hung on to the bitter end refusing to believe that anyone could do a better job than she could. On the other hand she was a very high E as her university subject (Chemistry at Oxford) and first job (a patent lawyer) demonstrated. Few individuals have the focus and attention to detail of Maggie T. What is not so well known was her H, but this was revealed in her business dealings with regard to her family.

On one hand the characteristics associated with P and E components are more often associated with males, as is the H component. People with high H component regard themselves as commercial, shrewd, and astute. Others see them as commission hungry, excessively materialistic, egocentric, name-droppers and flatterers.

> "...high M, D and A components are associated with female values."

This then gives us a behavioural basis for the glass ceiling. This term is generally used for the hidden barriers that prevent women making it into the top jobs as managers and executives of major companies. The ethos of the senior management of the majority of large companies may best be described as high H and P with a coating of N that provides the ethical veneer. To climb to the top of a large company you must be very commercial, very aggressive (particularly to your competitors and your peers) and shrewd. You should be able to flatter those above you and destroy those alongside you with neither group aware you are doing so. Finally you must be willing to accept the dominance of the organisation in return for its rewards. A person with high H and P will adopt this behaviour with an emotional intensity that others having weak or average H and P find difficult to comprehend.

Thus the organisation psychologists (who are often high A individuals) and personnel managers do their studies and produce their reports saying that good managers should have team building and nurturing skills. However, the books by practitioners usually describe H type management styles and organisation. For example, Al Dunlap's comment, *'If you want a friend, get a dog,'* is a classic Hustler statement in the way it sharply defines winning and losing behaviour. Andrew Neil (the former editor of the *Sunday Times*), in his book *Full Disclosure,* describes News Limited as an organisation revolving around the egocentric sun-king Rupert Murdoch. According to Neil, Murdoch is very commercial and opportunistic but suffers from having flatterers around him. Jack Welch, the former CEO of General Electric and named in 1999 by *Fortune* magazine as Manager of the Century, describes in his autobiography that his most successful personnel policy was to annually and automatically fire the poorest performing 10% of his management team. All this is typical Hustler behaviour.

So is there any hope for the female manager to break through the glass ceiling? Fortunately the answer is yes, mainly because of the growth of the service sector and realisation by organisations of the need to build long–term relationships with their various stakeholders. Individuals with high H and P components are not naturally good at providing service and building long-term relationships. The Hustler has a short-term, opportunistic management style, while the Politician finds it difficult to operate in partnerships, preferring to be the boss. People with high M and D components on the other hand are very good in service businesses. The M provides energy and people contact, while the D drives the need to provide service.

Already we are beginning to see the rise of the female manager beginning in occupations where client service is a key to success such as advertising, banking, superannuation, travel and tourism, though in industries such as mining and manufacturing female managers are still rare and likely to remain so. The emotional drivers to succeed in the larger manufacturing organisations are P and E while in the smaller manufacturing and mining companies the H is needed to provide the cost consciousness and entrepreneurial flexibility for success.

Leadership

Machiavelli in *The Prince* is widely regarded as the first writer to realistically describe leadership. His central insight was that successful leaders had to follow a special ethical code, one that differs from private morality or Christian ethics.

Machiavelli notes that even though everyone assumes princes should keep their word, experience shows that those who do not keep their word get the better of those who do. A prince should imitate the fox in cunning as well as the lion in strength. A wise prince should never keep his word when it would go against his interest, because he can expect others to do the same. A prince should do good if he can, but be ready to do evil if he must. In order to pull it off, you must be a good liar, but you will always find people willing to be deceived as long as their state is peaceful and prosperous.

> "A prince should imitate the fox in cunning as well as the lion in strength."

On the other hand, public image is most important because it is public support which is the firmest bedrock for a prince. A prince must always appear to be truthful, merciful, and religious, even if he must sometimes act in the opposite way.

Because you can expect other princes not to honour their word to you, you should not feel obligated to honour your word to them. This is Machiavelli's justification for deceit. Interchange leader for prince, and company for state and you probably have the best description of how most CEOs behave when working out how to combine principles with pragmatism. One CEO described this philosophy to me by saying you always had to remember that Ethics was only a county in England.

Daniel Goleman's book, Emotional Intelligence, puts forward the hypothesis (among others) that what makes a successful manager or employee is not intelligence or IQ, but EQ, or what Goleman defines emotional intelligence. Goleman supports this belief with a number of survey results but he also appeals to our common experience. Most of us know it is not the most intelligent of our peers who have turned out to be successful in life but people who appear to have other qualities.

Australian support for his theory, particularly for managers, has been provided by the Karpin Industry Task Force on Leadership and Management Skills Report. In 1994 the task force commissioned a research project where 100 experienced business managers were surveyed as to what they thought were the ideal management characteristics of the consummate manager. The results in Table 1 were illuminating – the survey results show that experienced managers consider people skills (defined as the ability to communicate with, train and motivate others) by far the most important, outweighing the IQ characteristic (the ability to solve complex problems and make decisions) by a factor of three to one.

Which management components make a successful leader?

Characteristic	Percentage saying ideal management component
Good people skills	75
Strategic thinker	58
Visionary	52
Flexible and adaptable to change	50
Self management	33
Team player	32
Ability to solve complex problems and make decisions	25
Ethical/high personal standards	23

With regard to the management of human resources, Goleman applies the EQ concept in the following way. All other things being equal, Goleman states that what drives an organisation's success is its culture; the culture in turn is driven by management. The key to culturally successful management is not IQ but their collective emotional intelligence or EQ. Successful organisations have managers and staff who have the four EQ factors, which are:

1. **Self-analysis** or the knowledge of one's own emotional drives,
2. **Self-management** or the knowledge of how to control one's own emotional drives,
3. **Social awareness**, defined as empathy or the ability work out other people's emotional drives,
4. **Social management** or the ability to manage other people by appealing to their emotional drives.

What makes the ideal leader?

What then is the make-up of the ideal leader and the habits they must develop to become management leaders themselves?

Jeffrey Pfeffer, Professor of Organisational Behaviour at the Stanford Business School, has developed an excellent model of leadership. Professor Pfeffer is widely regarded by his peers as perhaps the leading writer on organisational structures and leadership. In his seminal book *Managing with Power—Politics and Influence in Organizations* he identifies six characteristics of the leader.

1. Energy

The first common characteristic of leaders (as opposed to other people) is their energy and physical stamina. Leaders are the first in the office and the last to leave. Before they get to the office and after they leave they participate in other activities. During the day they continue to be active in a round of meetings. They are rarely sick.

2. Focus

Contrary to the popular view, perhaps pushed by the recruitment consultants, successful general managers are not general. Typically the people who become managing directors do so by focusing their energy and avoiding wasted effort. They succeed by focusing their efforts in one industry and generally one company.

3. Empathy

Successful leaders are aware of other people. They spend time thinking about the behaviour and personality of their colleagues and employees. They put themselves in other people's shoes.

4. Flexibility

To succeed as a leader it is necessary to be able to modify one's behaviour. Flexibility is essential to success, particularly for managers. People may not like flexibility in the abstract but they do like what it is able to accomplish.

5. Conflict

Leaders are willing to engage, when necessary in conflict and confrontation. Many people believe that to get along you go along. This belief is inculcated from an early age. However, leaders have discovered that conflict will often provide you far more power than pliability.

6. Team spirit

While confrontation is a key to success, another key—particularly in the larger organisation, is the ability to submerge one's ego and become a team player during one's career.

What then are the emotional drivers of the ideal leader? The first is the Mover or M component. The M component provides two characteristics of the ideal leader, energy and team spirit. Movers have far more energy than any other component and their desire to meet and communicate with people makes them good team players.

The second key component is the Politician or P component. This provides two more characteristics of the ideal leader, conflict and focus. P-style people naturally like to argue, they debate well and are usually forceful and articulate when expressing their views. In addition P-style people see life as a competition, and more importantly as one they have to win. Thus when they join an organisation they soon set themselves the goal of working their way to the top. They will become focussed in that aim and generate much emotional energy getting there. The P is Machiavelli's lion.

The final key component is the Hustler or H component. This provides the empathy and flexibility so necessary for a leader's success. H-style people spend a lot of time trying to work out what other people are thinking and planning to do. They put themselves in other peoples' shoes which, of course is what empathy is all about. While empathy can be a learned skill, Hustlers do it naturally. In addition to natural empathy, H-style people have natural flexibility. Graeme Richardson, a successful Australian politician who had a lot of Hustler component in his personality, defined it well when he said the key to political success was 'doing whatever it takes.' If that included having to be flexible about the truth, well that was a necessary evil. The H is Machiavelli's fox.

How do Australia's leaders stack up?

The most successful Australian Labor leader has been Bob Hawke. Under his leadership, Labor won four elections. Hawke is an excellent example of an HMP personality. Bob Hawke has demonstrated many of the characteristics of the Hustler component with his love of gambling, name dropping and financial opportunism since he left politics. His energy and desire to meet and talk with people was the stuff of a legend and also a strong indicator of high Mover component. Finally even after winning four elections he still believed he would win a fifth. This compelling desire to win is a good indicator of the Politician component. Bob Hawke was one of those rare individuals who combined all three key emotional components and in turn these emotional drives were a strong reason for his political success.

His successor, Keating had two of three necessary components—the H and the P. Keating is certainly flexible and he carried out some stunning U-turns during his political career. Edna Carew, in her book on Keating, describes him as 'charming', another Hustler trait, but also quotes other people's descriptions of 'arrogant' and 'aggressive'. These are characteristics of the P component, which is very strong in Keating. Few people would have the focus to last as long as Keating as Treasurer, put through the reform agenda, raise a leadership challenge, fail and then succeed. What Keating lacks is a high Mover component. That was his fatal flaw—he did not genuinely want to meet people, and his energy levels were low. Keating is not a team player; instead he was often described as being autocratic.

Howard has only one of the three usual leadership emotional drivers, the P component. He is articulate, good in debate and certainly persistent. His other two strong components are the Normal and Doublechecker. Howard comes across a compassionate, conscientious individual. The Labor party often tried to criticise Howard for being over-cautious and dithering. Howard certainly appears as if he dislikes making decisions which is in conflict with his P component. Ps generally like to make decisions. On the other hand, if a D decides to adopt a cause, he can attack it with an energy and persistence that surprises his colleagues. So it is with Howard when he attacked the issues of gun-control and tax reform.

The other strong component in Howard's personality is his Normal component. He dresses conservatively, comes across as a logical decision-maker, and even now after substantial media scrutiny is still regarded by many as 'Honest John'. Howard has since become the second longest-serving Prime Minister in Australia. He too has won four elections. A major reason for his success is that as he predicted 'the times would someday suit him.' The zeitgeist of the 1990s and early 2000s has been the Normal component: conservative, politically correct, conventional. Popular television shows, namely *Friends* and *Seinfeld*, were mainly about conventional people in a group situation.

The Art of Decision-Making

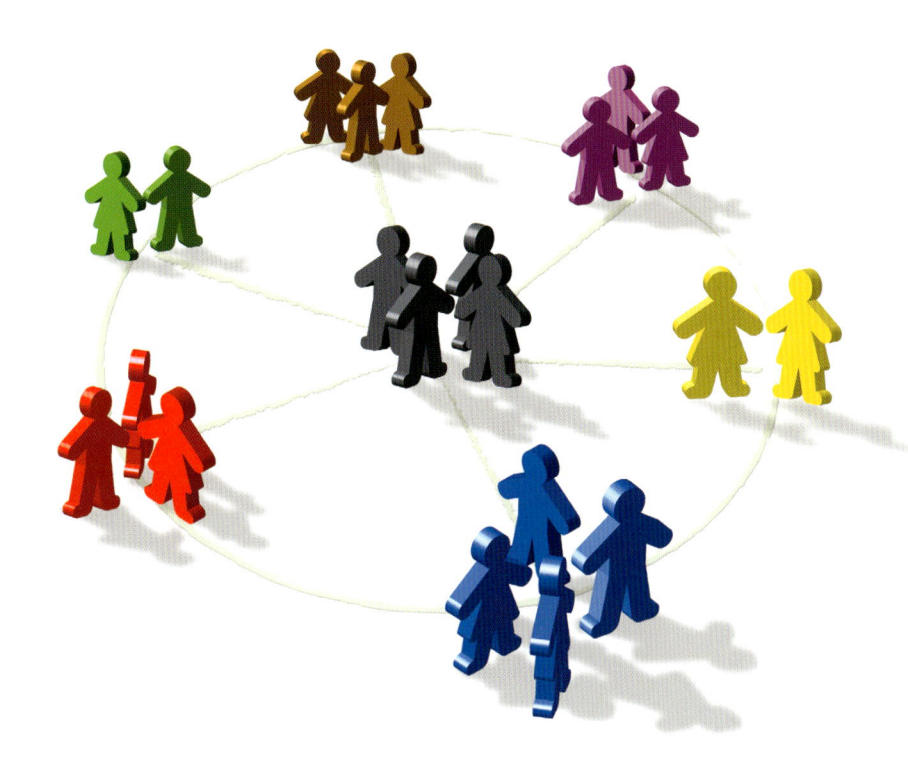

Introduction

In this section of the book we will consider five major plays as business case studies. Many of us may have seen at least one version of Hamlet or at least heard of it. As noted earlier we have chosen these five classics to analyse because we can all either see or read the plays, or rent a film version. Achieving the same depth of common knowledge about five different businesses or organisations is far more difficult.

Art, particularly the theatre, gives us a picture of what we are and what we want to be. Literature allows you to lose yourself; but it also allows you to find yourself. Management is about dealing with people and developing emotional intelligence. Thus using these five great plays to teach you people skills is not an abstract exercise but a useful pragmatic approach.

All five of these plays meet Aristotle's definition of a great tragedy. In each case there is one central character, the tragic hero, who moves from happiness to misery. The tragic hero is neither especially good nor bad, rather a person who we can relate to, but with certain defects such as excessive pride or procrastination. Creon, Brutus, Hamlet, Lear and Willy Loman all fit this profile. During each play, each of the heroes suffers from a lapse of judgement and makes a significant mistake.

- Creon decrees Polyneices must not be given a proper funeral.
- Brutus decides to join the conspiracy to assassinate Caesar.
- Hamlet refuses to kill Claudius while he is praying.
- Lear cuts Cordelia out of his will.
- Willy Loman gives his mistress new stockings.

From each decision, the hero suffers a terrible reversal of fortune and loses everything that he holds most dear including in some cases, his life. In every case we the reader can identify with these decisions and know deep down, that in similar circumstances and with similar personality defects we could do the same.

Each of the five chapters follows a consistent approach. After a plot summary, we will discuss the main characters in terms of their dominant components. Did they succeed or fail and if so, how and why? Then we conclude by attempting to draw some business lessons from the characters and the plays that will enhance your level of emotional intelligence.

Antigone

Sophocles, generally regarded as the greatest dramatist of ancient Greece, wrote *Antigone* over two thousand years ago. The play is the third part of a trilogy that tells the story of Oedipus, the Greek king who killed his father and married his mother, and who served as inspiration to Freud and his followers. *Antigone* is a play about choices and their consequences; the clash between family and work, traditional managers and the rebellion of youth. While set in 1200 BC these themes still make *Antigone* relevant to managers today.

Plot Summary for Managers

Antigone opens shortly before dawn outside the palace at Thebes, where Antigone secretly meets her sister Ismene. Together they grieve over the loss of their two brothers, Polyneices and Eteocles, who killed each other in a battle between Thebes and Argos. Polyneices fought for Argos, and Creon, the recently crowned king of Thebes, has ordered that his corpse remain unburied and that anyone who tries to perform funeral rites for him is to be executed. Antigone decides to defy the order.

A sentry guard then enters noting that no one likes the bearer of bad news as the bearer is often wrongly blamed. He tells Creon that someone has sprinkled dust on the body of Polyneices—an attempt at burial that violates Creon's decree. Creon is enraged and tells the sentry that unless the guards find the culprit, they will all be hanged. The sentry tries to convince Creon of his innocence, saying that the event was not his fault, but Creon is imperious and unyielding. The sentry leaves, saying in an aside to the audience that he will flee, never to return.

The sentry returns with Antigone saying she was caught trying to bury her brother a second time. When questioned by Creon, Antigone admits to both attempts at burial. Antigone fiercely defends her rejection of Creon's edict by claiming to act by the rules of justice and the gods, whom she says are supreme. Creon is equally unyielding, and claims Antigone's proud boasting of her deed is even more insolent.

Creon suspects that Ismene may be an accomplice in her sister's crimes. Ismene pleads for Antigone's life, reminding the king that not only is his prisoner part of his family (Antigone is Creon's niece), she is also betrothed to his son, Haemon. Creon refuses to reverse his judgment believing a good leader should not put his personal interests above that of the organisation he leads.

As Antigone and Ismene are led away, Haemon appears. At first, he seems willing to submit to his father's will. Creon talks about the importance of having loyal sons, the foolishness of taking an evil wife, and how being a good father to a family is the key to being seen as a good ruler. However, he goes on to note that disobedience is the worst of all evils, and that if people do not obey the law, order and discipline will vanish and a country will fall into anarchy.

With great caution and courtesy, Haemon tells Creon that the people of Thebes sympathise with Antigone. While claiming to have Creon's best interests at heart, Haemon suggests that Antigone should not be punished. Haemon also says that good leaders have the ability to acknowledge other points of view and accept advice. He also appeals to Creon's ego, asking that he let Antigone go free to show the people that he is a kind and forgiving ruler.

Creon is furious. He asks if his young son should advise a man Creon's age, and if the king should reward a wicked rebel. Haemon replies that the people of Thebes do not think she is wicked. The two men have a heated exchange, during which Haemon accuses his father of foolishness and Creon autocratically defends himself. Creon decides to bury Antigone alive with enough food and water so that the city itself is not held to blame for her death.

After Antigone has been led away, Teiresias, a blind seer, is brought before Creon. The prophet warns Creon that he is responsible for a sickness that has descended on Thebes. Teiresias expounds on the importance of taking advice, and says that a man who makes a mistake and then corrects it brings no shame on himself. Creon says this is balderdash that Teiresias has been bribed to concoct. Then Teiresias tells Creon that one of his children will die because Creon has violated the proper treatment of both the living and the dead.

Remembering that the old man's prophecies have never been mistaken, Creon finally changes his mind—but he is too late. He goes first to bury Polyneices but Antigone has already hanged herself. When Creon arrives at the tomb, Haemon attacks him and then impales himself. When the news of their deaths is reported, Eurydice, Creon's wife also commits suicide. Creon is alone and begins to rave, calling himself a rash, foolish man whose life has been overwhelmed by death.

Psychographic Profiles

Antigone

Antigone is the daughter of Jocasta (sister of Creon) and is both the daughter and half-sister of Oedipus who is both the son and husband of Jocasta. Antigone is dominated by the Artist component. Antigone is stubborn, idealistic and proud. She beats to a different drum. She is willing to sacrifice her life in order to bury her brother properly. She personifies the belief that family and human relations should be placed above politics.

Antigone is committed to her ideals. When her sister Ismene refuses to help her bury their brother, she ends their relationship, and, when caught, refuses to let Ismene share the punishment. When Creon tells her that she dishonours her dead brother Eteocles, she replies that Creon is dishonouring the gods by refusing to obey the unwritten laws of Zeus. Though she laments her fate, she first faces it defiantly, defying her role as a woman, which is to remain silent and follow Creon's edict. Later on in the play when her impending execution becomes a more concrete reality Antigone becomes more reflective and laments that she will never be Haemon's bride. Her complex emotions and strength of conviction make her character unique as a Greek woman and have rendered her a compelling heroine for centuries.

Creon

Creon is Antigone's uncle, brother of her mother, Jocasta. He was proclaimed regent (or ruler) after Oedipus's tragic fall from power. He has raised his sister's children as his own following Jocasta's descent into madness. He was to rule Thebes until Eteocles and Polyneices could rule together as adults. Unfortunately they were unable to agree on joint rule and plunged Thebes into civil war. After their deaths Creon was proclaimed king in his own right.

Creon is a big P. Like many Ps he enunciates principles for his staff to follow and then proceeds to break them himself. In his first speech he tells the elders that it is wrong to not give him bad news, as he will always be truthful about the situation to them. However when subsequently notified by a sentry that someone has defied his order that Polyneices is to remain unburied, he holds the sentry responsible until the culprit is caught. Creon is unbending and will not listen to the advice of his elders or Teiresias, the prophet. He is an autocrat. When faced with rebellion of any kind he immediately tries to suppress it. He also wants to hold on to power at any cost.

He is paranoid, suspicious and generally blames greed as the general motivation for disobeying his orders. When the elders suggest it is a god that has sprinkled the dust on Polyneices, he refutes it and says someone accepting a bribe did the deed. According to Creon, it is money that causes men to break the law.

Like many Ps who become leaders Creon identifies himself with the state or organisation. If he makes a rule, then disobedience means disrespect for the law, which means disrespect for the State, which means disrespect for Creon. The struggle with Antigone is not only about the need to obey the law. Creon, like many Ps when attacked, takes it personally and believes that his own manhood is at stake: 'I swear I am no man and she the man if she can win this and not pay for it.' Creon equates victory with masculinity and compromise with femininity. Antigone's gender makes it all the more important that Creon enforces his will. Creon's persistent refusal to obey what Antigone calls the 'unwritten laws' regarding honouring the dead leads to his downfall.

> "Creon is a big P. Like many Ps he enunciates principles for his staff to follow and then proceeds to break them himself."

Even the pleas of his own son Haemon, Antigone's fiancé, go unheard as he disowns him for being less of a man for defending his love. Of course, Creon's need to assert himself is made more urgent by the fact that Thebes has just barely survived a civil war. As the new ruler, Creon's authority is fresh and untested. Creon would realise that if he changed his decision to punish Antigone the citizens of Thebes might see it as special pleading. He would be favouring both the daughter of his sister and the fiancé of his son. Many people would weaken and change their minds but not a big P. He rejects his son's moderate advice out of stubbornness and an uncompromising attachment to a certain set of virtues. Creon's exaltation of order and love of authority, combined with the stubbornness and pride of a P, leads to an emotional hatred for any perceived threat to that order.

Ismene

Antigone's sister Ismene loves her sister and brothers, but refuses to help Antigone bury Polyneices. Ismene is a big D. She knows that family is important but is afraid to make wrong decisions. She reminds her sister that according to their role as women, it is not for them to decide what is right or wrong. When Antigone is caught, Ismene, like a true D, is willing to share the punishment, but Antigone denies her sister's involvement. Ismene is devastated by the loss of her brothers, but because of her D-based belief in her lack of status, she feels powerless to act on their behalf. Ismene acts as a foil for Antigone; she demonstrates a woman living according to tradition while Antigone is a revolutionary who governs herself according to a sense of personal empowerment and self-reliance.

Lessons for Managers

Don't exacerbate CEO disease: Telling Truth to Power

The natural isolation of the leader and the eagerness of subordinates to bring good news are natural causes of CEO disease. This is the information vacuum around a leader created when people withhold important (and usually unpleasant) information, which leaves the leader being out of touch and out of tune. It occurs when subordinates shovel nothing but good news onto the CEO's desk. 'How's it going?' the CEO asks. 'Great,' says the department manager. 'Good,' says the CEO. 'Keep it up.' Meanwhile, market share is eroding, key personnel are leaving, the sales spike was caused by a one-time event and front-line people are treating customers poorly.

Creon recognises that leaders have more trouble than anybody else when it comes to receiving candid feedback, particularly about how they're doing as leaders. In his opening speech Creon makes the point that a leader who does not listen to good advice is a failure, as is a leader who puts his own self-interest above that of his country. Creon implies that true loyalty is based on free discussion, and really loyal people will tell their ruler what they really think and feel.

However, telling the truth to power has never been easy. Some CEOs isolate themselves from bad news by punishing the people who bring it to them. The sentry chosen randomly by lot to tell Creon about the dust on Polyneices rapidly becomes an innocent victim along with his comrades. All too often those who attempt it often suffer badly.

Tantrums and tirades will discourage people from telling the truth. When his son, Haemon, tries to tell him the truth, Creon rejects him. Haemon is clever; he begins by praising saying he will follow his father's wise counsels. Yet when he argues for Antigone to be pardoned (to show Creon is a kind and forgiving ruler and saying the majority of Thebeans believe her to be innocent) he fails. Creon, like many Ps wants unquestioning loyalty to himself and whatever he may say or do. He first illogically refutes Haemon's arguments saying should a young son advise an older, more experienced father? He then dismisses Haemon's advice with the question: *'Should the city tell me how I am to rule them?'*

Similarly towards the end of the play Teiresias warns Creon that he is responsible for the sickness that has come down on Thebes. Teiresias says the gods are angry that the birds and dogs have defiled all the country's altars with the unburied body of Polyneices. Creon refuses to believe this explanation saying it is balderdash that Teiresias has been bribed to concoct.

Ps, like Creon, typically analyse situations in terms of the politics, not the truth or reason. Often emotions can become so strong that it is often impossible to have a rational exchange of ideas. High Ps typically either attack the underlying data saying that it is wrong or say the environment was poor and problems were caused by factors outside of management control.

Typically the only people who can tell the truth to a CEO with a high P are the non-executive directors who have sufficient wealth to be independent and are old enough not to worry about retribution.

Nobody likes the man who brings bad news

A great scene in Antigone occurs when Creon is about to be told that someone has sprinkled dust on the body of Polyneices. A sentry guard enters noting that no one likes the bearer of bad news and explains that he hastened slowly as he was afraid of the consequences. Creon asks what he is talking about and the guard describes the dust. As Creon is about to explode, the guard quickly goes on to say that every guard says he was not guilty, and that he was the poor person who drew the short straw to tell Creon. The sentry tries to convince Creon of his innocence, saying that the event was not his fault, but Creon is imperious and unyielding, believing money must have been involved.

Of course he soon returns, Antigone in tow, as now he is able to report good news, that they have captured the culprit who scattered dust on Polyneices.

For managers the lessons are obvious, if you have good news deliver it in person; if you have bad news, get someone else to deliver it or do it impersonally with a written memo. Remember the famous saying of the Greeks: *'Victory has many generals, defeat is an orphan.'*

You only have perfect wisdom at the end of your life

Managers must continually make decisions, and to succeed as a manager you must make the correct ones. Just as in life, choices in *Antigone* have their consequences. From the outset, Antigone's decision to bury Polyneices seals her fate, and leads to her capture and to her death. Similarly, Ismene's refusal to help Antigone ends her relationship with her sister. When Antigone is caught, Ismene is refused the honour of sharing her fate and instead is forced to live on alone, tortured by a loss of family and the knowledge that she may have made a cowardly choice.

Creon's unyielding government and his choice to ignore both the advice of Teiresias and the pleas of Haemon result in the loss of his son and his wife—as well as bad relationships with neighbouring cities. His refusal to bend to the will of the gods effectively ruins his life. All choices in the play—Antigone's, Ismene's, and Creon's—are made freely and are for apparently logical reasons. Antigone needs to bury her brother to satisfy 'unwritten law,' Creon needs to keep order after a civil war, and Ismene decides to follow the traditional role of women. Though all three characters make the choice that seems right to them, the results are disastrous: Antigone dies, Creon loses his family and power over the state, and Ismene is doomed to live the rest of her life alone, knowing that she did not try to help her family.

At the end of the play Sophocles says that we only have perfect wisdom at the end of our life. What he means is that during our lifetime we are confronted with many decisions—perfect wisdom means never making the wrong ones. The reality is that this state of perfection only occurs when we die, when we no longer can make decisions. Till we die we are always going to make mistakes.

The individual versus the organisation

Managers are continually faced with decisions about settling conflicts between the good of an individual versus the good of an organisation. Resolving this dilemma is perhaps the ultimate test of the leader, ancient or modern.

As the play begins, Creon is faced with a difficult task. You could consider Thebes as a family company with severe succession problems. The previous CEO discovers that he has unwittingly murdered his predecessor, who was also his father, and married his mother. Not surprisingly, he abruptly resigns for personal reasons. He believes he has implemented a winning succession plan by designating his two sons to jointly rule after he has finished. Unfortunately they fall out, fight each other and plunge the state into civil war. Ultimately they kill each other and Creon becomes the CEO. His first task is to create a climate of stability by re-establishing the rule of law. His first edict, that those who died fighting for the state should be given proper funeral rites while those who fought against it should not, appears fair. Unfortunately a close member of his own family disobeys this first edict. Creon is faced with a common management conundrum, should he overlook the transgression and stand accused of favouritism (or in this case, literally nepotism) or punish his niece according to his own rules.

The problem is compounded by Antigone's justification. She claims that she is acting as an agent of the divine will. Although she never justifies her actions by invoking her individual conscience, she maintains that the divine law is supreme; although she does remind us it is 'unwritten'. She says the knowledge of the divine will is derived outside of man's laws; it is her conscience that decides what she must do. Later, Antigone's conscience is validated by the gods themselves, through signs and the soothsayer Teiresias. However, till then Creon must decide what to do. His problem is that it is impossible to manage anyone if he or she can argue, on the basis of individually interpreted divine will, that certain rules are wrong.

The play is about the conflict between different values as much as it is about the struggle between two strong-willed people. Antigone is struggling against Creon, but she is also struggling for the rights of the individual. Creon is fighting Antigone, but he is also fighting against chaos, disorder, and the unravelling of the social fabric.

Creon's mistake is not that he puts lust for power ahead of the interests of the state; rather, Creon's weakness is an absolute confidence in a certain set of values. Again and again, he praises patriotism, loyalty to fathers, and civil obedience, elevating these values so highly that other kinds of justice are forgotten. Creon fears disorder; and in the wake of civil war, he needs to establish himself as a ruler.

Antigone's struggle is just as single-minded. Her devotion is to her brother and the dictates of her conscience, through which she claims she knows the 'unwritten' laws of God. But Antigone's actions are a threat to order and the institutions of law that protect the good of the people and provide justice. There are different kinds of justice at work in the play: there is the justice of man-made laws and institutions, symbolised by Creon, and the justice of the conscience and morality not written in law, symbolised by Antigone. Antigone proudly defies the laws of men, and suffers at the hands of those laws. Creon, in his pride, defies the laws of the gods and suffers at the hands of fate and divine retribution.

The art of compromise

In the play the conflict between Creon and Antigone is magnified because of their personalities. Creon is a P; he is decisive and understands the importance of strong, uncompromising leadership. However he has fixed opinions, is argumentative and believes he is weak if he changes his mind. Antigone is an A; she is passively stubborn, even if it is against her own self-interest. Neither is willing to compromise.

> **"Persistence is generally regarded as a virtue, but on the other hand there comes a time when it is necessary to pull the plug and either retreat or compromise. Flexibility is not always admired but it generally leads to better outcomes."**

For example, Creon states that the reason for his decree is that enemies must be treated manifestly worse than loyal citizens. However, he could easily distinguish between an enemy (Polyneices) and a patriot (Eteocles, his brother, killed in the same battle) by simple rites for the former and elaborate ones for the latter. Creon completely ignores the conflict between his decree and the hallowed custom of burial rites.

Similarly Antigone, aware of the law and the punishment, plans to bury her brother anyway. Her sister, Ismene, thinks the plan extreme, but can only counsel submission. Neither woman considers trying first to persuade Creon to amend the decree, which if successful, would make disobedience and its consequences unnecessary.

People often confuse stubbornness with leadership. However, intransigent leadership often produces tragic consequences. The story of Antigone is lived out today with remarkable frequency. Persistence is generally regarded as a virtue, but on the other hand there comes a time when it is necessary to pull the plug and either retreat or compromise. Flexibility is not always admired but it generally leads to better outcomes.

Julius Caesar

The murder of Julius Caesar is possibly the most famous assassination in history. In one sense it could be regarded as a play about a highly ambitious new CEO moving into a company that has a long tradition of participatory, democratic management. Some of the managers decide that the new CEO has to go, and convince an idealist to lead them. Indeed the play has been described as conflict resolution between an idealist (Brutus), an egotist (Caesar) and an opportunist (Cassius). A major theme of the play is the balance between the realities of public politics and the ideals and needs of private life. It has always been one of Shakespeare's most popular plays and even now has a modern resonance.

> "...the play has been described as conflict resolution between an idealist (Brutus), an egotist (Caesar) and an opportunist (Cassius)."

Plot Summary for Managers

The play begins in Rome in 44 B.C. on the Feast of Lupercal. Caesar has just defeated his rival, Pompey, in battle. He is now the most powerful man in the Roman Republic and is eager to become king. However, not everyone is thrilled at Caesar's victory, and in the market place two aristocrats, Flavius and Marcellus, chastise the people for their celebration and proceed to tear down celebratory decorations. Thus we are introduced to the key conflict of the play—the unrest between a popular dictatorship and a republican Senate who is disturbed by Caesar's rise to power and is willing to risk punishment to stem it.

Caesar thus has many enemies who are planning his assassination. When Caesar and his entourage appear, a blind soothsayer warns him to *'Beware the ides of March,'* (March 15), but Caesar is unconcerned.

Cassius attempts to manipulate Brutus into participating in the conspiracy to come, appealing to Brutus' love for his country and his devotion to freedom. Cassius argues that Caesar is too ambitious and must be assassinated for the welfare of Rome. Brutus hesitates until he learns from Casca that Marc Antony has tried to give Caesar a crown. Although Caesar refuses the crown three times, Brutus is so perturbed that he agrees to meet Cassius the next day. Cassius is determined to win Brutus to his cause. As Caesar's best friend and an honourable member of the Senate, Brutus legitimises the murder because he has no personal or political reason to kill Caesar other than his love for Rome. Cassius forges letters from citizens and leaves them where Brutus will find them. The letters attack Caesar's ambition and ultimately convince Brutus that killing Caesar is for the good of Rome.

For a month, Brutus struggles with the problem; and on the morning of the ides of March, he agrees to join the others. When the conspirators arrive, Brutus immediately takes charge of the situation, despite his previous reticence about participating. It is Brutus who refuses to let the conspirators swear an oath to kill Caesar, and remind them that shaking hands should be enough to bind them together. Brutus also rejects involving Cicero in the conspiracy despite his good and wise character. Brutus says that Cicero has a reputation for not finishing what he starts. Most importantly, Brutus rejects the notion of killing Antony, who Cassius notes is a 'shrewd contriver' whose enmity may subsequently hurt the conspirators. Brutus convinces Cassius to allow Antony to live because otherwise the conspirators will appear to be murderers killing too many people.

The conspirators escort Caesar to the Senate and stab him to death. Although the conspirators are successful in stopping Caesar from becoming king, they have little idea of how to proceed next, which is evident in their dealings with Antony and the Roman public. Antony, who chooses to flatter Brutus so that he will survive to avenge Caesar, shakes hands with the conspirators, indicating that he will agree to their plans. Brutus, anxious to justify his actions, tells Antony that there are reasons for Caesar's death and that Antony can speak at Caesar's funeral if he agrees not to speak against the conspirators. Cassius, is once again suspicious of Antony, and argues against Antony speaking but is overridden by Brutus. Cassius turns out to be correct in his assessment of Antony. Antony reveals in a soliloquy that he intends to avenge Caesar and throw the country into civil war.

Brutus addresses the agitated crowd and tells them why Caesar had to be killed. Then Mark Antony delivers his funeral oration and stirs the crowd to mutiny against Brutus, Cassius, and the others. The mob runs through the streets looking to avenge Caesar's death.

Brutus and Cassius escape to Greece where they raise an army and prepare to fight Octavius and Antony in a decisive battle. Cassius and Brutus disagree on military strategy. Cassius argues that they wait instead of attacking and make the forces of their foes tire themselves out by searching for them, but Brutus insists that they attack at Phillipi before Octavius and Antony are able to get more soldiers. When Cassius tries to make Brutus see his point, Brutus refuses to listen.

The battle begins and Brutus sees a weakness in Octavius' forces. Brutus' assessment of the situation is correct, but he leaves Cassius' army to the mercy of Antony. Cassius, believing the battle is lost, decides to have his slave Pindarus kill him. Brutus now realises he is defeated and commits suicide by his own sword rather than be taken prisoner back to Rome.

The play ends with the restoration of order, with Octavius and Antony becoming the joint rulers of Rome.

Psychographic Profiles

Brutus

Despite the play's title, Brutus is the central character of *Julius Caesar*. Julius Caesar dies halfway through the play while Brutus is alive till the final scenes. In private Brutus is compassionate for his fellow beings and fond of his wife and home life. Unfortunately his decision-making is often impractical and unrealistic and flawed due to his philosophical commitment to principle. At the beginning of the play, when he believes that Caesar has accepted the crown, Brutus admits that he has a conflict between his love of a republic and his love for Caesar. He goes on to say that if pushed he admits he loves his honour more than he fears death and will act for public good at any cost. The irony of the play is that he is pushed, he assassinates Caesar for the public good, but the end result for Rome is a more ruthless tyranny led by Antony and Octavius.

Brutus has high N and A components. He relies too much on logic and underestimates the power of emotions. He also believes himself to be more honest than anyone else and accordingly places himself on a pedestal: *'There is no terror, Cassius, in your threats, for I am armed so strong in honesty that they pass by me as the idle wind.'* Whether Brutus is totally honest is moot, but you do learn from this speech that Brutus is pompous.

> **"Here Brutus shows the tragic flaw of all As, their stubborn naiveté."**

Brutus does have a powerful imagination. In his first soliloquy he is unable to find any fault with Caesar's past behaviour, he projects his thoughts into the future and considers the possibility of Caesar accepting the crown, changing his nature and becoming a tyrant. He decides that to murder Caesar is the better course otherwise like an adder he would strike. Brutus resolves to think of Caesar *'like a serpent's egg, which hatch'd would as his kind grow poisonous, And kill him in his shell.'*

Like many idealists, Brutus justifies a decision on impractical, imaginary grounds and unwittingly creates the chaos that descends upon Rome after the assassination. Brutus confuses honour with treachery when he decides to kill Caesar for no existing reason. The road to hell is truly paved with good intentions.

Artists like Brutus beat to a different drum than the rest of us. The rest of the conspirators understand that what they are doing is murdering Caesar, and for them the reasons are personal. Brutus is different; he is killing someone for what they might do in the future, which is always a morally risky course. It certainly does not meet the test of doing unto others what you would have them do unto you.

> **"Throughout the play Brutus makes a number of decisions that are based on civil and moral grounds, yet are impractical and unrealistic."**

To justify the murder, Brutus internally converts it into a ritual sacrifice. Brutus almost literally states this intent when he declares: *'Let's kill [Caesar] boldly, but not wrathfully; / Let's carve him as a dish fit for the gods, / Not hew him as a carcass fit for hound.'* As soon as they have killed Caesar, Brutus tells each of the conspirators to bathe their hands up to the elbows in Caesar's blood and then besmear their swords. When the other conspirators propose that Mark Antony be killed as well, Brutus objects, arguing like a high N: 'Our course will seem too bloody. Let us be sacrificers, but not butchers.'

Brutus, as a high Normal, relies on reason and not emotion. He logically attempts to make the murder of Caesar seem like an honourable deed, a ritual sacrifice. In his oration at Caesar's funeral, Brutus, in response to those who question why he killed Caesar, argues rationally that his actions indicate: *'Not that I lov'd Caesar less, but that I lov'd Rome more.'*

Brutus is reputed to be a competent, admired political and military leader, but after the assassination makes a number of mistakes. It is at Brutus' behest that Mark Antony is spared, and it is Brutus who permits Antony to address the crowd after he departs from the scene. Here Brutus shows the tragic flaw of all As, their stubborn naiveté. He quickly accepts Antony's offer of friendship and his promise not to stir the ground, despite the warnings of Cassius. Brutus also errs militarily; his strategy of taking the offensive plays into the enemy's hands, and at the crucial moment, he gives the command to advance too early. Throughout the play Brutus makes a number of decisions that are based on civil and moral grounds, yet are impractical and unrealistic. He is deemed a public man because he chooses to follow noble and idealistic principles in an environment that recognises them only to take advantage of them. Finally, like many As, Brutus suffers from self-deception, for he truly believes that he can purify Caesar's assassination by regarding it as a ceremonial sacrifice.

At the end of the play, Brutus against the stoic principles that he has followed all his life, commits suicide, an act he earlier described as cowardly and vile. Ironically this action wins him honour among his friends, and the praise of his enemy, Antony, for the first and only time in the play.

Julius Caesar

Caesar is a high P. Early in the play he refers to himself in royal terms: *'I hear a tongue shriller than all the music/Cry 'Caesar.' Speak. Caesar is turned to hear.'* Although Caesar has a great deal of power, he is not a king and his reference to himself as Caesar belies his great belief in his own power. He then listens to the soothsayer telling him to beware the Ides of March and arrogantly dismisses the soothsayer as a dreamer.

Just before his death Caesar again shows the high-handed arrogance and fixed opinions of the P. Metellus Cimber pleads for the return of his banished brother, but Caesar rejects his fawning, comparing the grovelling behaviour of Metallus to that of dogs. When Brutus and Cassius offer their support for Metellus Cimber, Caesar associates himself with the North Star and with Mount Olympus saying he will be constant and unwavering on this issue.

Caesar's own words and actions, as well as those of other characters in the play, can provide insight into his character. *'The eye sees not itself but by reflection, by some other things,'* (self-knowledge is difficult and we know ourselves only by the reflection of perceptions of others). Most of the characters in the play who discuss Caesar are his enemies and they of course describe his flaws, in particular his over-ambition, arrogance and egotism which are the classical flaws of a high P.

For example, Caesar (like all Ps), is susceptible to flattery. Decius Brutus, who persuades Caesar to go to the Senate even after he has promised to Calpurnia he would not go, describes Caesar thus: *'When I tell him that he hates flatterers, he says he does, being then being most flattered.'*

Cassius tells Brutus how Caesar was boastful about his swimming prowess and how he challenged Cassius to join him in a swim across the Tiber on a day when the river was churning and turbulent. Caesar almost drowned and had to be rescued by Cassius. Likewise, Cassius recalled a time during one of Caesar's military campaigns in Spain when Caesar fell victim to a 'fit' in which he was shaking and feverish. Cassius sums up Caesar's behavior as that of *'a sick girl.'* Nevertheless Cassius also realises how powerful the public face of Caesar is. While the private Caesar is a superstitious man plagued by illness, the public figure is a demigod or a superman who in the words of Cassius, *'doth bestride the narrow world like a Colossus.'*

On other hand, Caesar pulls Mark Antony aside and tells him of his mistrust of Cassius. Caesar asserts, however, that he does not fear Cassius. Thus Caesar demonstrates that he is to some degree a good judge of character; he is suspicious of Cassius, who indeed poses a threat to him.

Caesar is a brave soldier. One of his more famous statements is that: *'Cowards die many times before their deaths, The valiant never taste of death but once.'*

However, his excessive courage combined with his high P is his fatal flaw and makes him blind to the precautions that ordinary men would take in politics.

Cassius

Cassius is a high H. His principles are adaptable, and because he has his price believes all men have theirs. A good example of this is in his first soliloquy (where the dramatic convention is that the actor is speaking the truth). Cassius notes that while noble minds should keep company with other noble minds lest they are seduced, no one is so firm that he cannot be persuaded to change his course. Flexibility is a characteristic that we may not admire, but it does get results.

Cassius is willing to use deceitful means to achieve ends which he judges to be honourable. For example, Cassius sends Brutus forged letters, ostensibly from Roman citizens, which highlight Caesar's alleged ambitions. Cassius thus hopes to persuade Brutus to join the conspiracy.

Cassius, like all high Hs, has an overriding interest in money. Brutus says to Cassius in the famous quarrel scene: *'You yourself are much condemned to have an itching palm, To sell and mart your offices for gold to undeservers.'*

Cassius sees this as a necessity, and does not hesitate to finance both his and Brutus' armies by plunder, bribes, and selling commissions. He would argue the situation is too desperate to adhere to moral principles.

Cassius is a realist who is not superstitious. For example he tells Brutus: *'The fault, dear Brutus, is not in our stars, But in ourselves that we are underlings.'*

Throughout the play Cassius reveals himself to be an accurate judge of other men and their abilities. He sees through Antony who thinks like himself. However his perspicacity fails when he deals with Brutus. Normally Cassius has good judgment, however he unfailingly defers to Brutus' decisions in various matters throughout the course of the play. The one group of people that high Hs cannot understand and manipulate are the high As.

Antony

Antony is another high H with considerable M. His athletic nature, as well as other virtues, are noted by Brutus who states that Antony is: *'given to sports, to wildness, and much company.'* Caesar also points out that Antony: *'revels long o'nights.'* (This view of Antony as a drunken dilettante is what spares him from being an additional target of the conspirators.) When the conspirators are considering whether to kill Antony along with Caesar, Trebonius agrees with Brutus in the assessment that Antony is somewhat of a playboy, and not a threat to their plans. The two reassure the others that there is nothing to fear in Antony.

After the assassination Antony, like a true H, is able to conceal his emotions. When Brutus promises to explain to him the reasons why Caesar was killed, Antony shakes hands with the conspirators stating that he does not doubt their wisdom. After the conspirators leave Antony with Caesar's body, he delivers his first major speech in the play: a soliloquy in which he vows vengeance.

Towards the end of the play, in what is know as the proscription scene, Antony, Octavius, and Lepidus—who have formed a political alliance—are compiling a list of Romans who will be killed or executed. At Lepidus' request, Antony agrees to the death of his nephew in exchange for the life of Lepidus' brother. In this scene we see a true H in action: pragmatic, expedient and untainted by moral considerations. Typically the flaw of the H is that they will sacrifice the long term for the short term. In the next play *Antony and Cleopatra* Shakespeare describes how Antony sacrifices everything for an affair with the Egyptian Queen.

Lessons for Managers

Beware of tunnel vision

In the previous chapter on Antigone we warned prospective managers about the threat of CEO disease. Organisations and their leaders thrive only when essential information reaches those who need it. If this information is not sent (the CEO disease), then problems will occur. In Julius Caesar we see the counterpoint—tunnel vision. Information is Caesar fails to recognise and act on critical information. All managers, by dint of their position, have an obligation to seek and listen to reality.

Caesar was a superb and intelligent military leader who would know there were no victories without first-rate intelligence. Caesar should have realised that fateful morning that something was up; the warnings were everywhere. He was warned by a soothsayer to: *'Beware the ides of March.'* An owl hooted unnaturally during the day, and a lion ran through the streets. And then there was Calpurnia's nightmare. Caesar's wife begged him not to go out after she dreamed that his statue poured blood: *'like a fountain with an hundred spouts . . . and many lusty Romans came smiling and did bathe their hands in it.'*

Why did Caesar fail to recognise and assess the information that flowed all around him. Why did he fail to recognise the threat presented by the other conspirators. This self-defeating form of tunnel vision is a common mistake of managers, particularly those with a successful track record.

Over a six-year span, Sydney Finkelstein, a professor of management at the Tuck School of Business at Dartmouth University, studied why businesses founder. He wrote about his findings in *Why Smart Executives Fail: And What You Can Learn From Their Mistakes.* One way that organisations isolate important information is by imposing rigid rules about who can speak to whom. Another way is for managers to refuse to listen to staff. Ps like Julius Caesar are particularly prone to this failure. If they are very intelligent like Caesar they will have built up a track record of being usually right. This can lead to hubris and become a fatal flaw. Leaders must develop the habit of asking themselves if they know all they need to know. They need to question their assumptions, and they need to encourage everyone else in the organisation to do the same thing.

How ambitious should a manager be?

Immediately after Caesar is slain, Brutus proclaims to his fellow conspirators that *'ambition's debt is paid.'* Ambition is in fact a central theme of the play. Its centrality is underscored by Mark Antony's use of the word 'ambition' in his funeral oration for Caesar. He asks the crowd the rhetorical question: *'Did this in Caesar seem ambitious?'* after recounting that Caesar enriched *'the public coffers and wept when the poor cried.'* If this was 'ambition' Mark Antony argues, then it should be made of *'sterner stuff.'* The mob tacitly assents to Antony's argument that Caesar was not ambitious.

Caesar, as Shakespeare clearly shows, was in fact ambitious. He is lured by Decius into coming to the Senate by the prospect of his being crowned king. Ironically, though, the most ambitious of the play's characters is not Caesar nor Brutus, but Mark Antony, who exploits the situation at hand to become a member of the ruling triumvirate along with Julius Caesar's heir apparent Octavius (Augustus Caesar).

Ambition, in the conventional meaning of the word, is the cause, but not the primary motive, of the conspiracy against Caesar. For all of the conspirators except Brutus, envy and resentment toward Caesar fuel their individual decisions to assassinate this 'colossus.' Envy is most evident in Cassius, who complains:

*'And this man
Is now become a god, and Cassius is
A wretched creature, and must bend his body
If Caesar carelessly but nod on him.'*

Cassius measures himself against Caesar and finds no reason that he should not hold the same power as this self-proclaimed 'god.' There is, however, no explicit plan for Cassius to seize the rule of Rome once Caesar is dead. The minor conspirators of the plot are generally motivated by dissatisfaction with Caesar's high-handed treatment of them and by personal grievances.

Brutus, however, is ambitious in the sense of being divided between two visions of the future. Brutus has no complaint against Caesar as he is, but fears what he might become if the people and the Senate crown him as Rome's king. *'He would be crown'd; / How that might change his nature, there's the question,'* as Brutus poses it to himself. Unlike Cassius and the others, Brutus does not act out of personal envy or resentment over past wrongs, but out of fear for the future of the Roman Republic. For the sake of Rome, Brutus takes personal responsibility for the murder of its ruler, bathing his hands in Caesar's blood as an open acknowledgment of his deed. But after the regicide is done, Brutus continues to be plagued by doubts and haunted by great Caesar's ghost. Trying to straddle the present and the future, Brutus acts irrationally, making a series of self-defeating political and military blunders.

> **"One of the lessons of the play is that while we can all be ambitious, if we are to rise to the top of an organisation we need to have the people skills to get there."**

One of the lessons of the play is that while we can all be ambitious, if we are to rise to the top of an organisation we need to have the people skills to get there. Those who have power and want to keep it must be able to ingratiate themselves to the masses. It is because Caesar and Antony are master politicians that they are able to succeed and overcome otherwise popular figures like Pompey and Brutus. Those who can not control public opinion will finish like Pompey and Brutus; replaced by those who are more popular.

How do you remove a poorly performing CEO?

One of the major issues *Julius Caesar* deals with is the overthrow of a CEO. In this play Shakespeare raises the question of whether this is ever justified and if so, under what circumstances. At the time Shakespeare was writing, a commonly held view on this topic was that the overthrow of any ruler—good or bad—was morally wrong. (Kings and Queens in particular were considered second only to God—to dispose of them would have been the same as disposing of God.)

Dante's *The Inferno* written between 1308 and 1321 describes the ten levels of hell where each level of sin is associated with a different level. For example murderers are placed at a lower level than robbers. In the poem, Dante (an Italian poet) put Brutus and Cassius (along with Judas) in the lowest level of Hell as punishment for their regicide. However Machiavelli, another famous Renaissance writer, had a different view. He discussed the causes that would lead people to seek to overthrow a ruler and argued that some situations applied, such as failure to defend the kingdom, or failing to keep civil order.

The same arguments apply in modern times. The system that has evolved in the modern corporation is that there is a Board of Directors who continually review the performance of the CEO, and if the performance is deemed inadequate, then moves to appoint a successor. Of course there are problems with this approach. Does the Board really know what is going on? Certain individuals, particularly HPs with low Normal can be oppressive and dictatorial with their staff, engage in unethical practices, yet at the same time convince their Board that they are compassionate, empowering leaders. Fortunately the composition of public Boards does change with retirements due to age, fixed length terms, etc. A good, independent non-executive director, if approached by an internal whistleblower will treat the matter with concern. Alternately, private companies, or companies controlled by a major shareholder such as the entrepreneur who built the company, have much greater problems with rogue CEOs. The only solution for a manager caught in this situation may be to move on to another organisation.

Sell to the heart, not to the head

One of the great principles of selling is that you must sell to the heart and not to the head. You gain support for your arguments not from logic but from emotion. The advertising industry is based on this simple principle. If you look at the structure of any advertisement or great sales presentation you will see that it follows a simple acronym: AICDA, which stands for Attention-Interest-Conviction-Desire-Action. In five simple steps you:

1. gain the *attention* of the prospect;
2. then develop *interest* with a simple message;

3. build *conviction* with evidence and repetition;
4. develop an emotional *desire* for the product;
5. try to translate the desire into a call to *action*.

The speeches by Brutus and Antony are the critical turning points of the play. Caesar has just been murdered, and the conspirators have yet to justify their action to an angry Roman public. Antony, meanwhile, has sworn to avenge Caesar's death while publicly agreeing to the conspirators' demands. The outcome of the entire play depends on who can gain the trust of the mob. Because Antony, like his mentor Caesar, has the greater emotional intelligence, he is able to successfully persuade the Roman public to turn against the conspirators and sweep them out of the city.

Brutus is the first to speak to the crowds after the assassination of Caesar. He speaks first because, as he has previously explained to Cassius, he hopes to gain an advantage with the crowds by showing Caesar respect:

> *'I will myself into the pulpit first*
> *And show the reason of our Caesar's death.*
> *What Antony shall speak I will protest*
> *He speaks by leave and by permission*
> *And that we are contented Caesar shall*
> *Have all true rites and lawful ceremonies.'*

This demonstrates Brutus' motivation not only for the next scene but also for the act of killing Caesar—he wants to do what is honourable and good for Rome without seeming like a butcher. This is also the same reason that Brutus refuses to allow the conspirators to kill Antony. Cassius, by contrast, does not concern himself with appearing savage, but tells Brutus that allowing Antony to speak at Caesar's funeral is not a good idea, as Antony may be able to sway the public. Brutus then makes the mistake of believing that he can control Antony's influence by dictating what Antony may say at the funeral:

> *'You shall not in your funeral speech blame us*
> *But speak all good you can devise of Caesar*
> *And say you do't by our permission,*
> *Else shall you not have any hand at all*
> *About his funeral. And you shall speak*
> *In the same pulpit whereto I am going,*
> *After my speech is ended.'*

Brutus mistakenly believes that by not allowing Antony to say anything bad about the conspirators and that by making Antony speak second, he will be able to diminish the influence Antony may have over the people. Antony obeys both instructions in his funeral oration but is still perfectly capable of turning the mob against the conspirators.

Brutus' begins his speech by saying that they should listen to him because he is honourable, which should engender respect for him. He then makes an appeal to the crowd's logic: *'Censure me in your wisdom, and awake your senses that you may the better judge.'* This appeal is critical to Brutus' argument. The entire premise of the conspirators' plot to kill Caesar is that Caesar must die because he may become a tyrant. They have no proof that Caesar would become one, but they infer that he will because he has the power to do so. This argument is logical in nature rather than emotional, and it is what has led Brutus to the conspiracy even though he loves Caesar. In order for the crowds, who also love Caesar, to accept the actions of the conspirators they must, in Brutus' opinion, hear and believe the argument of the conspirators and repress their emotions, which is why Brutus asks them to use their own logic in listening to his justification. In order to remind the crowds why they should put aside their love for Caesar, Brutus then reminds them that he too loves Caesar, probably more than any other, but that even Caesar is not more important than the love of Rome. At this point, Brutus is making a patriotic appeal to love of country, which is often considered a 'higher' love than that of an individual. Brutus combines love of country and logical thought by asking the public if they would have preferred to be slaves than for Caesar to die. He urges the Romans to appreciate all of the benefits that Caesar brought to Rome, but not to forget that they might have become slaves because of Caesar's ambition. Brutus then ends the first section of his speech with a series of questions to indicate that none of the Romans have been offended or harmed by the death of Caesar. All of these arguments demonstrate what Brutus himself believes to be important: namely honour, freedom, and love of country.

The second section of Brutus' speech occurs as Antony is bringing the body of Caesar out from the Capitol. Brutus reminds his audience that he has not offended or harmed anyone, and that Caesar would have eventually harmed them all because of his ambition. He also reminds them that they will all receive the benefit of Caesar's death, namely freedom from tyranny. All of these arguments are logical, and the mob appears convinced. They even go so far as to demand that Brutus be named Caesar, showing the same fickleness that moved them from support of Pompey to Caesar in the first place. Brutus does offer two dramatic actions to reinforce the good opinion of the crowd at the end of his speech. First, he offers to kill himself if his country needs him to do so (which the crowd begs him not to), and then he demands that the crowd stay and listen to Antony's funeral oration while Brutus departs alone. This first action is emotional yet underscores the logic of Brutus' arguments because the whole point of killing Caesar is that it is best for Rome. The second action, leaving before Antony's speech and demanding that the crowd stay, is intended to show Brutus' unrealistic faith in his own arguments. By insisting that the public stay for the funeral, Brutus appears to be fair and honourable, qualities that he has been attempting to put forth during his speech. And for the moment, the crowd believes him.

Unlike Brutus, Antony recognises the gullibility of the Roman public and turns it to his advantage while at the same time obeying Brutus' strictures about not speaking against the conspirators. Although it seems as if the Romans cannot be swayed after hearing Brutus' speech, Antony knows that the crowd easily changes opinions and manipulates them by appealing to their emotions and to their own greed. Unlike Brutus, Antony is not concerned with what is 'honourable'—he only wants to avenge Caesar's death and kill the conspirators. Antony begins his speech by demonstrating he is on common ground with Brutus:

> 'I come to bury Caesar, not to praise him . . .
> The noble Brutus
> Hath told you Caesar was ambitious.
> If it were so, it was a grievous fault,
> And grievously hath Caesar answered it.'

This search for common ground is the first principle of all persuasion. It is how you get **attention**. Antony appears in agreement with the conspirators. He begins this way because the crowds have already been convinced by Brutus' arguments, and Antony must lure them back bit by bit.

Recognising that the crowds believe Brutus to be honourable (as Brutus spends so much of his speech reminding them that he is), Antony continually uses the statement: *'Brutus says he [Caesar] was ambitious, and Brutus is an honourable man.'* This is the next key tactic in persuasion. Develop **interest** in the buyers by finding a simple theme they can understand.

The next step is to build **conviction** in the buyer by repetition of the message. The first time Antony uses this statement is when he mentions to the public that the conspirators have allowed him to speak. The second time he uses it is after he notes that Caesar was a good and just friend, reminding the crowd that he too was close to Caesar. Antony then proceeds to subtly attack Brutus' assertion that Caesar's ambition made him dangerous to Rome. He reminds the crowd that Caesar brought a great deal of money through captive ransoms, he cried for the poor and assisted them, and three times refused the crown that Antony offered him at Lupercal.

The crowd is now interested and convinced because Antony is talking about them and events they can relate to. Gradually the crowds begin to question if Caesar was as ambitious and tyrannical as Brutus said, particularly when they reflect on all of the benefits he brought to Rome.

Having stemmed the hostility of the crowd, Antony turns to motivating them to attack the conspirators. After reminding the public once again that Brutus and the conspirators are honourable men, he mentions the topic of Caesar's will. This is the next step in selling, building **desire** by appealing to a key emotion. Of all the emotions, self-interest is the one horse in the race that is always trying. As soon as the word 'will' is mentioned everyone stops and asks the same question. Is there anything in it for me? Instead of reading it immediately, Antony stirs the crowd's curiosity by only mentioning that if he were to read it, the will would upset them because they would realise Caesar's love for his countrymen. When the mob begins to demand that Antony read the will, he continues to refuse for the crowd's own 'benefit' which, of course, makes the crowd more insistent. By doing this, Antony has not only restored the love of the crowd for Caesar, but he has done so by getting the crowd to make him do it instead of openly betraying the conspirators.

> "This simple acronym: Attention, Interest, Conviction, Desire, Action or AICDA is the structure behind many successful advertisements and presentations. Antony's speech is one the first great pitches based on the AICDA acronym and well worth studying."

Antony is now ready to move to the final step of the presentation—**action**. He shows Caesar's body to the crowd. However, now that Antony has motivated their love for Caesar, their curiosity and their greed, the sight of Caesar's mangled body moves the crowd towards vengeance and rioting.

Although Antony may well have manipulated the crowd enough to destroy the conspirators by this point, he ensures his success by a few last tactical decisions. First, he once again reminds the crowd that the conspirators are honourable and will have answers for the points that have come up during his funeral speech. The effect of this reminder, of course, is to anger the crowd further and make them less likely to listen to the conspirators, which occurs.

Antony also says that he is not an orator as Brutus is, and has no power to convince the crowd of anything.

> 'I come not, friends, to steal away your hearts,
> I am no orator, as Brutus is;
> But (as you know me all) a plain blunt man.'

This appearance of being weak in comparison to Brutus makes Antony seem pitiable while Brutus appears ambitious and powerful, the two traits Brutus has spent so much effort to eradicate. Once again, Antony, a true H, is not concerned with the truth of his statements. Anthony has become a fox and learnt a key skill of leadership, the ability to fake authenticity.

Finally, Antony ensures his success when he reads Caesar's will, which gives every citizen money and leaves all of his property to the state for public use. This final reminder of Caesar's love for his people, resulting in a monetary benefit for every citizen, stirs the greed in the crowd and starts the rioting. Antony is able to succeed in his attempt to turn the Roman crowd against the conspirators despite their earlier support of Brutus, because Antony tailors his appeals to what matters most to the Romans—their own self-interest.

This simple acronym: Attention, Interest, Conviction, Desire, Action or AICDA is the structure behind many successful advertisements and presentations. Antony's speech is one the first great pitches based on the AICDA acronym and well worth studying.

Lessons for Life

Does the end justify the means?

The crux of *Julius Caesar* is a moral issue that is as topical today as it was in Caesar's day. It revolves around the question of whether the killing of a leader (such as Saddam Hussein) is justifiable as a means of ending (or preventing) the tyranny of dictatorship and the loss of freedom. Brutus strikes Caesar down is the name of liberty, fearing that absolute power and Caesar's view of himself as more than a mere mortal, will enslave Rome to the will of a single man. In doing so he throws Rome into civil war, and raises an important question; is rule by a tyrant, however intolerable, better than a country being thrown into disorder?

Brutus fears that the people will anoint Caesar as their absolute monarch. The violent actions of the base mob confirm his view of the common people as an irrational body capable of surrendering their liberty (and that of Rome's nobles) to Caesar. Brutus wants liberty for himself and his Senator colleagues but not for the people. By contrast, the other conspirators, while agreeing with the arguments of Brutus, have their own reasons for removing Caesar. Again this is resonant with our own times. The question has been raised whether the supporters of US President Bush's removal of Saddam Hussein were in favour to promote democracy as claimed or to gain access to oil.

While a Roman future without Caesar temporarily prevents tyranny, it yields an even worse outcome from the standpoint of the Republic; civil war. Just before inciting the mob to action, Mark Antony foresees the carnage ahead and predicts:

'And Caesar's spirit, ranging for revenge
With Ate by his side come hot from hell,
Shall in these confines, with a monarch's voice
Cry 'Havoc!' and let slip the dogs of war,
That this foul deed shall smell above the earth
With carrion men, groaning for burial.'

Thus it comes to pass. Seventy Senators (the layer of middle management that keeps an organisation going) are killed and Rome descends into civil war. Again this is a situation repeated throughout history and is resonant with our own times.

Hamlet

Hamlet is widely regarded as one of the greatest plays of the English language. There is the apocryphal story of someone who, after seeing the play for the first time, remarked to his partner: *'How can anyone say that was good; all Shakespeare did was string a lot of familiar sayings together!'*

It is said that every actor wants to play Hamlet, and judging by the number of *Hamlet* film and TV productions it looks as if the wish may be fulfilled. However it is as a management text that we want to consider the play.

Imagine yourself in the following situation:

Over the past thirty years your father has started and gone on to build one of the country's top 100 companies. It is the largest business in the city where you live and employs over 80% of the workers living there. Your father, a top athlete in his youth and someone who has kept himself fit and healthy, is well respected and known for his energy, integrity, and vision. You are the heir apparent, having worked in the business every summer while you are undergoing formal training. You have just completed your final program, a two-year full time MBA course at Harvard, and you have taken a two-week trekking holiday in South America with some of your fellow students where you have been out of contact.

When you arrive home you discover the following:

- Your father is dead and no one can tell you how he really died.
- His brother, who you always thought was a pompous ass, has become CEO.
- The employees, who used to disregard your uncle now speak glowingly about his qualities.
- Your mother has married your uncle and you now have a stepfather.

- The culture in the company has suddenly changed. Before people were open and enthusiastic, now they are guarded and working nine-to-five.

This is the situation that Hamlet finds himself in when he suddenly returns back to Denmark. So the next time you think you have problems, reflect on the struggles that Hamlet faced.

Plot Summary for Managers

The play begins on the battlements of Elsinore, a castle in Denmark. Prince Hamlet of Denmark is urged by his father's ghost to avenge his murder at the hands of the dead king's brother, now King Claudius. To make matters worse, Claudius has re-married the widow, Queen Gertrude, Hamlet's mother. Hamlet is unsure whether the ghost is his father or a goblin from hell and whether its intentions are wicked or charitable but decides to believe the ghost. The ghost calls upon Hamlet to kill his uncle but at the same time not to seek to punish his mother.

Action now shifts to the Danish Court where Claudius and Gertrude are in discussion with Polonius, the King's aged chief adviser, and his son Laertes. Denmark is under threat of invasion from young Fortinbras, who seeks to regain lands lost to Hamlet's father. Claudius announces that he is sending ambassadors to Norway to ask that Prince Fortinbras be restrained. Then he agrees to Laertes returning to France.

In the meantime, Hamlet decides to feign madness with his family and friends, including his girlfriend, Ophelia, sister to Laertes and daughter to Polonius. A major issue during the play is whether Hamlet is acting crazy or is actually slightly mad. Both Polonius and Laertes warn Ophelia against Hamlet's amorous advances. Claudius directs Gertrude to try to learn the cause of Hamlet's odd behaviour; they suspect it is the result of the old king's death and their own recent marriage.

Ophelia then appears saying that Hamlet seems to be mad. Polonius immediately concludes that this is because Hamlet is lovesick for Ophelia who has been acting aloof to Hamlet in accordance with her father's instructions. He rushes off to tell Claudius and Gertrude but Claudius demands more proof. Polonius proposes that he and the King conceal themselves and spy on Ophelia and Hamlet. They both see Hamlet spurning Ophelia and both conclude Hamlet seems slightly insane. The King then reveals to Polonius his plan to send Hamlet to England.

Hamlet seizes the opportunity presented by a traveling troupe of actors to use a play as a mechanism to trap the King. Hamlet asks them to put on *The Murder of Gonzago*, which replicates the supposed murder of a king and to which he will add some lines. At the moment of murder, Claudius acts as if a man found out and storms out of the hall followed by the Court.

Soon after, Hamlet delays killing Claudius because the King is at prayer and Hamlet does not wish to send him to heaven instead of hell. When Gertrude meets with Hamlet as Claudius has directed, Polonius hides in Gertrude's bedroom to eavesdrop on the conversation. Hamlet arrives and he begins to argue with his mother. There is a cry behind the curtain and Hamlet believing it to be Claudius, draws his rapier and stabs the body behind which turns out to be the spying Polonius. She is appalled at the murder but then is stunned when Hamlet accuses her of killing a king and marrying his brother. Hamlet then begins to reproach his mother when the ghost reappears, which only Hamlet can see. His mother, shocked by the murder of Polonius, is now convinced her son is mad.

Claudius, on hearing of the death of Polonius and realising the rapier thrust was meant for him, decides that he will send Hamlet to England with a letter asking the King of England to kill Hamlet as soon as he arrives. Claudius summons Hamlet and tells him he must sail to England for his own safety. Hamlet eventually escapes, and returns to Denmark.

Meanwhile Laertes has returned from Paris. He too is seeking revenge for the murder of his father Polonius. Laertes raises a mob and invades the palace. Then Laertes sees his sister Ophelia who herself has become mad and is beside himself with enraged grief. Nevertheless Claudius skilfully persuades Laertes to calm down, and that they should jointly seek the murderer of Polonius.

He concocts a plot with Laertes to kill Hamlet by arranging a fencing match between the two. He proposes that Laertes fight with an unblunted sword so it looks like an accident. Laertes agrees but suggests that he goes further and dips his sword in poison. Then Claudius adds a contingency plan by having a cup of poisoned wine at the match for Hamlet to drink.

Later in the court the plan is put into action and the fight begins. Hamlet scores the first hit and Claudius attempts to get Hamlet to drink the poisoned cup but Hamlet refuses. The fight resumes and again Hamlet scores a hit. This time Gertrude unwittingly tries to get Hamlet to have a drink; she fails and then drinks from the cup herself. The third time they fight Laertes wounds Hamlet with the poisoned sword, but then the swords are exchanged and Hamlet again wounds Laertes; this time with the poisoned sword. Gertrude then collapses but manages to cry out that she has been poisoned. Hamlet orders that the castle's doors be locked and the treachery be exposed. Laertes realises his time his short and tells Hamlet that both he and Hamlet are about to die from poison and that Claudius is to blame. Hamlet then plunges the poisoned foil into Claudius finally getting his revenge. As Hamlet dies he asks Horatio to tell his story to the world. Drums are heard and Fortinbras arrives just in time for Hamlet to prophesy and approve him to be King of Denmark.

Psychographic Profiles

Hamlet

Hamlet is dominated by the D component. The first question that Claudius asks of Hamlet is evidence: *'How is it that the clouds still hang on you?'* Hamlet himself recognises his melancholy. His first soliloquy begins: *'Oh that this too too sullied flesh would melt, thaw and resolve itself into a dew.'* Ds are loyal individuals and of all the personality types are the most dutiful towards the family. It is difficult to imagine a more terrible situation for a D than to have your father murdered and your mother apparently marrying the murderer. He describes the earth as *'a sterile promontory'* and the air as *'a foul and pestilent congregation of vapours.'* He changes his view of mankind from being *'like an angel in apprehension'* to a *'quintessence of dust.'* He concludes his first soliloquy like a true D: *'Man delights not me; nor women neither.'* On the other hand Ds are also cautious individuals and throughout the play Hamlet's strong sense of caution causes him to be indecisive. Indeed some critics have suggested his procrastination is the result of cautious analysis of his position.

Hamlet is also a big A. He is introverted and individualistic, but has a strong imagination combined with a bent towards philosophy. Like many Artists Hamlet has a strong fashion sense. Ophelia described Hamlet thus: *'The expectancy and rose of the fair state, the glass of fashion, and the mold of form.'* Hamlet while an idealist when he was younger is now disillusioned. Like many introverted Artists he is also lonely and disassociated. He only really confides in one person, Horatio.

Of course this is understandable. Hamlet would have had a comfortable childhood and at university his idealism would have flourished. Suddenly he is confronted with subjects killing kings, brother killing brother and mothers making incestuous marriages. Not surprisingly Hamlet becomes depressed and disaffected. His problem is that his dominant Artist component makes him an introverted, solitary individual unable to trust his friends and make joint plans for revenge.

Critics have put forward various theories for Hamlet's procrastination:

1. Hamlet doubts whether the ghost is real.
2. He is only convinced that Claudius killed his father when the actors arrive and perform the play.
3. Hamlet is schooled in philosophy and religious thought and is aware that reacting emotionally to his intense hatred of Claudius is not acting rationally.
4. Revenge is against the teachings of the Bible. *'Vengeance is mine saith the Lord, I will repay.'* It is not you or I who should seek revenge; but God.

A better explanation is that Hamlet is an AD, the combination that is most likely to procrastinate. Doublecheckers do not make decisions because they are scared they might be wrong; Artists hate to make decisions about people because it may show that they are insensitive. Hamlet also has a low Hustler. Claudius describes Hamlet as: *'Most generous and free of all contriving.'* His moral scruples work against him particularly when he is in a corrupt environment.

Claudius

Claudius has many of the characteristics of the successful CEO. He is energetic and decisive, yet understanding of human behaviour and flexible. He is a classic HMP with the H being the strongest component. Claudius is driven by self-interest. A true H, Claudius knows that he is engaged in deceptive behaviour. *'How smart a lash that speech doth give my conscience.'* However he is very good at manipulating people particularly when under pressure. For example he manages to turn the enraged Laertes from attacking him to attacking Hamlet. He does this by promising Laertes that if any guilt should attach to him, then he would forfeit both his kingdom and his life and Laertes will be given complete satisfaction. Yet like many HMPs Claudius has a very high opinion of himself, as when he pompously tells Gertrude not to try and restrain Laertes: *'There is such divinity doth hedge a king, that treason can but peep to what it would.'* His P is also strong and like all Ps if wronged seeks retribution. His advice to Laertes in the same scene is particularly telling: *'Revenge should have no bounds.'*

The fatal flaw of Claudius is that his N is weak; thus he has few morals or ethics to temper his self-seeking behaviour. The high H/low N combination provides an explanation of why some people are evil and have *'some vicious mole of nature.'*

Shakespeare puts forward three explanations as to why some people suffer from this defect:

1. The first explanation is genetic. The defect is inherited. In this case the person does not bear responsibility; the individual is a victim of fate.

2. The second is some form of substance abuse such as alcohol or drugs which causes the individual to lose his self-control and act in an anti-social manner.

3. The third is due to a faulty temperament. The individual suffers from an *'o'ergrowth of some complexion,'* that often breaks down the *'pales and forts of reason.'* (A pale is a stake which is part of a protective fence. Beyond the pale first referred to a secure fenced area around civilised Dublin and where the barbaric natives lived outside.) Here the individual suffers from a strong emotional drive that overcomes a person's rational and social behaviour. This explanation is particularly perceptive and conforms with the high H/low N interpretation proposed earlier.

Note that this explanation is not genetic. While the level of H is innate, the level of N depends on the individual original make-up combined with his upbringing and social milieus. Typically over time the N level gradually grows.

In the play three characters are typically regarded as foils to Hamlet: Horatio, Fortinbras and Laertes. Foils are characters that are used to illuminate the personality of the main character of a play.

Horatio

Horatio dominates the first scene and survives the carnage of the last scene. He is Hamlet's closest friend, a scholar and accomplished youth. He is rational in his approach, and is best described as a phlegmatic Stoic. He is not afraid of the ghost when it first appears. Unlike Hamlet, he is not prone to emotional analysis nor does he dwell on philosophical issues. He is able to see wrong and tries to right it with a straightforward action. Horatio has a strong E component.

However Horatio is also a D. He has the habit of putting himself down. At one point he describes himself as 'truant' by nature, a person who does not meet his responsibilities. This is definitely not the case; during the play he is a good and loyal friend to Hamlet. One reason for this is the common D component. The golden rule of temperament is that we like people who are like ourselves.

Hamlet immediately counters Horatio's self-abuse by saying that he would not allow anyone else to say such a derogatory statement and that it is unfair of Horatio to force Hamlet to hear such comments. People who put themselves down are not only their own worst enemy but they also imply the listener is impotent. On the other hand Horatio does possess the characteristic that Hamlet should have to avoid his tragic downfall. Horatio maintains the proper balance between *'blood and judgement.'* He does not let his emotions overrun his rationality.

Fortinbras

Fortinbras is a stark contrast to Hamlet; he is a classic MP. He is decisive and active. He is a valiant General; leading an army across Denmark to fight for a small plot of land he believes rightfully belongs to Norway. Hamlet is not just envious of Fortinbras, but realises that he too could be active and decisive. Towards the end of the play Hamlet remarks to himself: *'How all occasions do inform against me and spur my dull revenge.'* Hamlet compares himself to Fortinbras and realises that while Fortinbras started off in a worse position (his father had been defeated in battle by Hamlet's) he has overcome his difficulties, while Hamlet has been procrastinating. Hamlet concludes with a vow: *'O, from this time forth, My thoughts be bloody, or be nothing wort.'* This concept of a person being an **informant** for another is a problem than many young managers face. Often their peers subconsciously realise that the manager is achieving something they want but did not have the confidence to strive for themselves. They have failed to realise that *'If it is to be; it is up to me.'*

Laertes

Laertes is the third foil. Like Hamlet his father is murdered (by Hamlet) and he seeks revenge. However, unlike Hamlet, Laertes has high M and H and low N. He is high-spirited and Shakespeare early in Act I contrasts Laertes wishing to return to Paris with Hamlet brooding in the castle dress in inky black. Laertes is quick to action and emotion as when he leaps into Ophelia's grave. However he can also be unscrupulous, as when he quickly adds poison tips to the plan devised by Claudius for the rigged sword fight between Hamlet and himself.

Polonius

Polonius, the father of Laertes, is a familiar character in many organisations. He is the long-serving adviser, who by use of flattery and spying has working himself into a position of power. A number of critics have said that Shakespeare based Polonius on Lord Burleigh, the Lord Chamberlain for Queen Elizabeth, who also ran her secret service. Polonius is an HP, pompous, bombastic, and full of self-importance with low self-control. He loves the sound of his own voice, and his statement that … *'brevity is the soul of wit,'* is full of unconscious self-irony. His famous advice speech *'Neither a lender nor a borrower be . . .'* is a prime example of his hypocrisy. The speech ends with the admonishment *'To thine own self be true,'* which is not how Polonius behaves himself. The speech itself is given just before Laertes is about to head off to Paris.

As any parent knows, giving advice to their children is generally a waste of time, but particularly when they are off on a trip. It is better to wish them luck and tell them you will miss them. Polonius does the opposite and gives advice, which he continues to do all through the play. While the speech of Polonius is ethical, his actions during the play are the opposite. He sends a spy to Paris to check on his son, and he uses his daughter as bait for Hamlet. After he and Claudius eavesdrop on Hamlet and Ophelia, and Claudius wonders if Hamlet really is lovesick for Ophelia, Polonius, obstinately sticking to his theory, proposes that they use Gertrude as bait. This action subsequently leads to his demise. It is an interesting irony that his murder is more important to the play than the murder of King Hamlet, for it is the source of Laertes' rebellion which in turn drives the alliance between Claudius and Laertes which eventually leads to the death of many of the characters.

Lessons for Managers

The fish first rots from the head

'Something is rotten in the state of Denmark,' is one of the more famous quotes of Hamlet and this is one of the key dilemmas of the play. The ethical culture of an organisation is set by the moral basis of its leader. If the CEO is corrupt his morality will spread through the organisation. Claudius is a leader that has gained power on a morally corrupt basis. In the first act Claudius justifies his taking power by saying he has the support of the Royal Court. Also there are external forces in play with Fortinbras considering the invasion of Denmark. These two arguments, internal support and external danger are constantly used by morally corrupt CEOs to justify their staying in power. They assert with no proof that the staff respect and support them and that current circumstances are such that leadership change would be imprudent.

How then does an ethical person survive in an organisation that is morally corrupt? Typically an employee is faced with two choices, either leave the organisation or sit and wait for the leader to change.

Hamlet is in a much more difficult position. He is the heir apparent so he is unable to leave the organisation. Moreover, he cannot sit and wait because he has apparently been commanded by his father's ghost to seek revenge. On the other hand if he does seek revenge he is in fact committing regicide which is not exactly the strongest basis on which to start a new reign (as we have seen in *Julius Caesar*).

Claudius is also in a difficult situation. Typically if a new CEO has a rival, one of his first steps is to have the rival fired. This is not an option for Claudius. He cannot have Hamlet banished because as he admits Hamlet is popular with the people and if he punishes Hamlet for the murder of Polonius, Hamlet's supporters may well rebel. Claudius and Hamlet are in a Mexican standoff. Both want the other to disappear but neither can publicly carry out such an act. Claudius tries various forms of subterfuge such as sending Hamlet to England with a sealed message to the English King to behead Hamlet, and setting up a fixed sword fight between Laertes and Hamlet. In the end Claudius is found out and he destroys himself.

Incorrect assessment of people's emotional drives can lead to incorrect decisions or even worse – inactivity

Hamlet is perhaps the most intelligent character in the English canon. His soliloquies are rightly regarded as pearls of the English language. His high A and D make him super-sensitive to people. However the critical decision of the play is his refusal to kill Claudius when he appears to be praying. Hamlet believes Claudius is being devout and if he slays Claudius while he is praying he will send Claudius to heaven. However, we the audience, know that Claudius is not praying for forgiveness or repenting, indeed he is doing the opposite.

More importantly, Hamlet's inability to make decisions has terrible consequences. People who are indecisive generally have low self-esteem and are self-preoccupied. They blame others. Hamlet curses the world but in reality is cursing himself. He is like a sailboat being pushed by the winds about him.

Life improves with practice. If you make decisions it will dispel the sense that the world is against you. If you make a mistake you will at least learn from it and more importantly realise that mistakes are not so important. Life goes on. If you seek perfection and refuse to take risks you will fail. You also cannot expect to have limitless options. At the end of the play Hamlet finally learns the critical lesson:

> *'We defy augury. There is special providence in the fall of a sparrow.*
> *If it be now, 'tis not to come;*
> *If it be not to come, it will be now;*
> *If it be not now, yet it will come.*
> *The readiness is all.'*

What this passage means is that there is no point listening for people who claim they know the future (augurs were official Roman soothsayers). Fate acts in mysterious ways and even a sparrow falling can have an effect (like the butterfly's wing in chaos theory). The opposite result you expect from a decision will often occur; however what is important is to be ready to make decisions and to actually make them. Often the decision needs to be a compromise. Also decisions can often be reversed. However, what is necessary is to be ready for whatever happens and to realise that what happens is often the opposite of what you expect.

King Lear

King Lear is perhaps the most complicated plot devised by Shakespeare. *King Lear* is interesting in that after it was written, it became the play most changed by subsequent directors. The original play was considered too bloodthirsty and irreligious. For several centuries after Shakespeare's death theatre-goers saw a play where Cordelia married Edgar and lived happily ever after with her father.

In modern times Lear is much more resonant. We are now far more aware of how cruel man can be to his fellow men. Also we in the western world are less religious. Churchgoing has declined and many more people are either agnostic or atheists. Lear is a pagan play and as such is fatalist in its approach.

There is a good argument to suggest that by the time Shakespeare wrote *King Lear* he had become much more humanistic in his beliefs. For those unfamiliar with the play the following summary may be of use.

Plot Summary for Managers

Lear, king of ancient Britain, decides to divide his kingdom among his three daughters: Goneril and Regan, the wives of the Duke of Albany and the Duke of Cornwall, and Cordelia, his youngest and favourite. In an attempt to give the 'largest bounty' to the one who loves him most, the king asks for his daughters' expressions of affection. He receives embellished speeches of endearment from the older two, but Cordelia modestly speaks the truth, angering her father who disinherits her and banishes her forever. Lear divides her third between Goneril and Regan. Trying to intercede on Cordelia's behalf, the Earl of Kent also is banished. The King of France marries Lear's dowerless daughter. Lear then announces that he will spend alternate months with each daughter accompanied by 100 of his knights, beginning first with Goneril and her husband, Albany.

The subplot then begins, concerning the old and superstitious Gloucester and his two sons, the good-natured but naive Edgar and his illegitimate brother the witty and calculating Edmund. Edmund, wishing to gain his brother's inheritance, forges a letter supposedly written by Edgar saying that he wishes to kill his father. The gullible Gloucester believes the lie and promises Edmund the inheritance. Edmund continues the falsehood by persuading Edgar to go into hiding, which he does, adopting as a disguise a mad beggar, Tom of Bedlam.

Lear's plans to live with his two older daughters are immediately thwarted when Goneril turns on him, reducing his train of followers by half. In shock from her ingratitude, Lear decides to seek refuge with Regan and her husband Cornwall. Instead of admonishing her sister for her actions as Lear expects, Regan is harsh with him, suggesting that he apologise to Goneril. Heartbroken and rejected, Lear totters out into the storm with only his Fool and Kent to keep him company. Kent, who is now in disguise, finds refuge in a hovel for the king, who has been driven mad by his suffering. There they meet Edgar, disguised as Tom of Bedlam, hiding in fear for his own life.

In the meantime, Cornwall gouges out Gloucester's eyes, calling him a traitor and telling him that his bastard son, Edmund, was the informer. A servant then kills Cornwall. Still in disguise Edgar leads his blind father to Dover. Edmund, in command of the English army, defeats the French, taking Cordelia and Lear as prisoners. As Gloucester is dying, Edgar reveals his true identity to his father. Edgar kills Edmund, but cannot save Cordelia whom Edmund has ordered to be hanged. Lear dies, grief-stricken over Cordelia's death. Rivalry over their love for Edmund leads Goneril to poison Regan and then stab herself. Albany, Kent, and Edgar are left to restore some semblance of order to the kingdom.

Psychographic Profiles

Lear

Lear has a dominant Politician component:

- Like many Ps, Lear enjoys being flattered. The play begins with Lear asking each of his daughters to tell him how much each loves him, and rewards the two who flatter him and disinherits the one who doesn't.
- Lear demonstrates how mulish a P can be by remaining fixed in his opinions and refusing to change his mind about Cordelia by denying her a dowry when she is asked to choose her husband.

- He is also vengeful in that when his trusted adviser for many years, Kent, argues the case for Cordelia, Lear quickly banishes him.
- He is egotistical throughout the play referring to himself constantly and having a very self-centred view of life.
- He is very much concerned with the trappings and status symbols of power. For example when Regan suggests to Lear that he return to Goneril, who had dismissed half his train of 100 knights, he refuses on any terms but his own. He demands that the 50 knights be reinstated.

For a CEO, high Politician is a necessary component. CEOs need to make decisions and Ps can take them. More importantly as anyone knows who has been in a managerial position, once you have taken a difficult decision, the second guessing starts. If you do not have a strong P, you may waver and change your mind. Then people will accuse you of inconsistency.

However for a king, inheriting a position of power, the problem is more complex. Surrounded by courtiers and repeatedly told that they are 'Every inch a king,' a prince with high P can become delusional about his potential power. A good example from history is King James II, the last catholic monarch of the United Kingdom. Even though his father, Charles I, was beheaded and the country had been through a civil war and been a republic for eleven years during his lifetime, James II still tried obstinately to re-introduce Catholicism as an official religion. As predicted by his brother, James II was deposed within four years of his coronation.

Like many Ps, Lear does not have high self-awareness. His daughter, Regan, says of Lear: 'He hath ever but slenderly known himself.' Interestingly, during the play, particularly when Lear is wandering on the heath during the ferocious storm two things happen. First of all Lear slowly and gradually starts to lose his N component. This happens to many people as they approach old age (and remember some scholars have estimated Lear to be around 80) and often is described as entering a second childhood. On the other hand Lear progressively gains more understanding about his own condition and his self-awareness gradually increases. He first asks: 'Who is it that can tell me who I am?' and then goes on to describe himself: 'I am a man more sinned against than sinning.' Both these statements reek of self-pity. However as the play progresses Lear gradually learns about himself and becomes more aware of other people. In a very famous passage Lear is wandering about in the ferocious storm, abandoned and impoverished. He then realises how little the powerful understand the sufferings of the weak and cries out:

> 'Poor naked wretches, wheresoever you are,
> That bide the pelting of this pitiless storm,
> How shall your houseless heads and underfed sides,
> Your looped and windowed raggedness, defend you,

> *From seasons such as these? O I have taken,*
> *Too little care of this! Take physic, pomp;*
> *Expose thyself to feel what wretches feel.'*

At this moment Lear's self-awareness begins to grow.

Cordelia

Cordelia is a big A. As we now know people with high A component tend to be quiet, reticent and stubborn. Cordelia fits the bill perfectly. She only has 111 lines and those she speaks simply and quietly. When given the opportunity by her father to change her tune she adamantly refuses. The stubbornness costs her both her inheritance and her dowry. However by the end of the play Cordelia too has learnt the same lessons of humility that Lear has had to discover.

Gloucester

Gloucester is a big D with low H and P. He is affectionate, and enjoys the pleasures of life (he fathered an illegitimate child). However he is credulous and completely superstitious, believing totally in astrology. His blinding by Cornwall and his discovery of Edmund's terrible nature makes him pessimistic to the point of suicide, but like many Ds who talk about suicide he never goes through with it. He also goes through a transformation of self-awareness.

Edgar

Edgar undergoes perhaps the most marked development of any character in Lear. At the beginning he is as credulous as his father, Gloucester. His H is very low and like many people with a similar lack of H cannot believe that there are people who are evil. He makes the mistake that many people make, of believing that all people are the same and deep down like themselves. The problem is that Edgar is a good person who also believes that gods are always just. Such gullible people are easily fooled by Hs and this happens in life again and again.

Edmund thus tricks Edgar into fleeing home too easily. However by surviving as a mad fool, Edgar learns about life and how to endure. He learns to become cheerful in adversity and helpful in a practical way. While Lear's N gradually goes, Edgar's N gradually grows. By the end of the play he becomes self-reliant and the King of England.

Edmund

Edmund is one of the great Hustlers of literature and well worth study. He is calculating, lies convincingly and has the brilliant ability to fake authenticity as in the scene when he pretends to be hiding a false letter. He is also a total realist. Such people are rare and are generally successful in life. Edmund has good self-awareness, good empathy and instinctively knows how to make others act and decide emotionally.

Edmund divides the world into winners and losers. The winners are atheists and materialists, and are not bound by moral or ethical considerations. The losers are weak and use the gods as excuses for their own bad behaviour. Edmund firmly places himself in the winning camp when declares in his first soliloquy: *'Thou, Nature, art my goddess.'* On the other hand, he puts both his brother and father in the losing camp, even going so far as to betray his father.

Edmund is physically handsome and like all Hs would dress himself well to show off his best features. Like many Hs, Edmund has a subtle self-deprecating humour and also refuses to fool himself. As he is dying, he learns of the death of both Goneril and Regan, and says: *'I was contracted to them both: all three now marry in an instant.'*

Goneril and Regan

One of the major attractions of *King Lear* is that it is a play about family relationships. Typically in a three child family, the eldest is the most argumentative, the middle child the more manipulative, while the youngest is typically spoilt. During our lifetime we all become involved in family relationships (particularly parent-child) and one of the attractions of *King Lear* is how Shakespeare dramatises the characters in ways that resonate with our own experiences.

The two older sisters are very much kindred spirits to Edgar and that is in part an explanation of their mutual attraction. It is not just sexual attraction. We like those who are like ourselves. They are both Hs, suspicious of the motives of others. Goneril also has more P and is the more paranoid.

> Albany: *'You may fear too far.'*
>
> Goneril: *'Safer than trust too far.'*

As typical Hs Goneril and Regan are always calculating their opportunity for the main chance and continually trying to improve their position. A good example is when both negotiate with their father about reducing the number of knights in his entourage. Of course their position is readily understandable. While many of us have parents living with us, very few would be able to cope with an entourage of cronies every night.

Both understand the power of flattery and use it well, particular in the initial scene when Lear is handing out his kingdom. They are realists and also divide the world into winners and losers and both try to keep themselves in the winning camp. They both start as potential winners because of birth, but still keep striving to improve their position. They are under no illusions about their own good fortune: *'... he always loved our sister most; and with what poor judgement he hath now cast her off grossly.'*

Goneril has more M and P than Regan; she is more active and decisive. She is the first to argue against her father. She is willing to get rid of her husband, a Duke, in order to marry a potential king and is willing to poison her sister to succeed.

Reagan probably has more H than her sister. She follows and then tries to outdo others in cruelty. A typical reaction is when her husband, Cornwall, decides to put Kent into the stocks till noon and she cries *'till night.'*

Lear gradually realises that his initial favouring of Cordelia was correct and to throw his lot in with the two older sisters was a great mistake. He asks: *'Is there any cause in nature that makes these hard hearts?'* not realising that the amount of H component is genetic and not externally caused. Fathers throughout time have suffered with recalcitrant children, as managers with recalcitrant employees. Lear bitterly notes: *'How sharper than a serpent's tooth it is to have a thankless child.'*

Lessons for Managers

If we think of the court of Lear as head office for Corporation England, what do we have?

- An arrogant, opinionated CEO near retirement who wants to delegate the work but keep the pomp and ceremony.
- A divisional head has been promoted above his level of competence, but keeping his position through loyalty.
- A designated successor who stubbornly beats to her own drum.
- A second tier of plotting managers, who are totally driven by self-interest who ultimately destroy themselves by infighting.

For many of those who have worked in large corporations at least one of the above situations will sound familiar.

King Lear teaches us first about management succession. It might be regarded as a play about a successful CEO nearing retirement who wants to hand over power and how he chooses his successor. Few managers, who have climbed up the organisation getting and keeping power, are able to easily give up a fraction. As the manager nears retirement, it becomes particularly difficult. This is truer for owners who have built up a successful business. Delegation to newly appointed successors often proves difficult if not impossible. Typically the best solution is for the retiring CEO to leave the organisation and then sit on the Boards of non-associated companies. However, far too often the mistake is made of keeping the CEO on the Board and making him or her Chairman or President.

> "...the succession decision is among the most subjective and intuitive a manager makes. If a manager does not have the self-awareness to understand his own temperament nor the empathy to understand the emotional drivers of others, the decision may prove wrong."

Moving on is only part of the problem; the other side is deciding who moves up. Picking a successor is rarely easy. In some public organisations the CEO is now cut out of the decision of picking his successor, the job being done by a subcommittee of the Board comprising Non-Executive Directors with an executive search firm as advisers. However in a family-owned organisation the problems of succession are even more difficult and every generation provides to the media examples of organisations being torn apart by feuding siblings.

In the play Lear nearly destroys his organisation by first not choosing a competent successor and then secondly impeding the effectiveness of the new management by not letting go of the reins of power.

Finding a Competent Successor

Lear begins by deciding he will decentralise his organisation by dividing it into three parts and giving each part to a daughter. This first decision is flawed in that it automatically creates rivalry. For countries, it often leads to civil wars as happened recently when Yugoslavia broke up into warring states. He then goes on to compound the mistake by removing Cordelia from the succession and leaving only the two sisters, Regan and Goneril. With three potential successors there will always be a balance of power element in any conflicts. With only two potential successors mutual antagonism quickly appears. This occurs in Lear where the two daughters move from an alliance against their father to a rivalry over Edmund that becomes so vicious they plot to kill each other.

Lear then made the mistake of wanting to do another screen of his candidates. His selection criterion was not competence or experience, but who could best flatter him. Unfortunately this is not an artificial situation. Most CEOs have a high amount of the P component and Politicians want to be flattered. On the other side Hs know how to flatter. Hs are charming and cunning. Hence all too often you will see high P CEOs choosing H managers as their successors.

On the other hand, managers who quietly get on with the job, are ethical and tell it like it is, who in fact do follow all the rules of 'leadership' professed by modern management texts find that they are overlooked or like Cordelia, retrenched with a small redundancy payment.

Choosing a successor is not easy. Typically when asked how it is done, managers will say that they used criteria such as track record, leadership qualities, no known criminal record, etc. The reality is that the succession decision is among the most subjective and intuitive a manager makes. If a manager does not have the self-awareness to understand his own temperament nor the empathy to understand the emotional drivers of others, the decision may prove wrong. A common situation, particularly with managers who have a high H component and low N, is to choose replacements that will poorly perform. Doing this makes their own tenure look even better.

Another common case occurs when you have a manager, who has not been performing because of the wrong temperament fit for the job. An example would be a manager with high P component leading a group of creative engineers developing a new product. The manager may well think he has done an excellent job and then choose a replacement similar in temperament to himself and so compound the problem.

Increasingly large organisations are using psychological profiling to gain a better understanding of the people they are hiring and promoting. It is a technique that small organisations can easily adopt.

Moving on

In the play Lear claims that he wants to retire. Many CEOs make this claim but few do it so poetically:

> '... 'tis our fast intent
> *To shake all cares and business from our age,*
> *Conferring them on younger strengths, while we*
> *Unburthen'd crawl toward death.'*

The reality is that Lear does not hand over power. He demands office facilities from both his daughters that he plans to alternate monthly. He also keeps a retinue of 100 knights who are to be paid by the realm. Note that this is not a small burden and 100 knights would include horses, squires, etc. Lear also refuses to give up the title of King.

> *'I do invest you with my power,*
> *Pre-eminence, and all the large effects*
> *That troop with majesty. Ourself by monthly course,*
> *With reservation of an hundred knights —*
> *By you to be sustain'd — shall our abode*
> *Make with you by due turn. Only we shall retain*
> *The name and all th' addition of a king.'*

This proves to be as unworkable in Lear's organisation as it does in a modern one. Within weeks Lear and his retinue have caused so much turmoil that Goneril and Regan, not unreasonably, are forced to take action. Lear, with his high P, refuses to listen, curses them and then in a rage, rushes out onto the moors into a ferocious storm that sends him mad.

Lear did not really retire and this refusal to move on generally proves to be a disaster to trying to run the organisation. New managers will find it impossible to do their job well if they have previous managers hanging around, second guessing decisions, and even stepping in and changing them. Subordinates will become confused and the new managers will find that their authority is undermined.

This is true for management but even truer for CEOs. Why is this? The reason is inherent in the job of the CEO. While the job of the CEO has been defined in many ways, one of my favourites is that the CEO is the person who is empowered to break the rules. Organisations survive by developing rules and processes. However, individual cases can require different treatment. The classic example is the granting of clemency to a murderer condemned to be executed. In those US states where capital punishment is legal the right to reprieve a murderer is granted to the CEO. You need to have someone who has the right to break the rules but at the same time has the authority to enforce them. On the other hand you cannot give this right to more than one person or else confusion will reign.

This problem is particularly true when children inherit a business. The family owner finds it very difficult to hand over. Often odd organisational arrangements are made such as annually rotating CEOs. One family business went so far as to have two brothers act as CEOs on alternating weeks.

A successful executive transition appears to comprise three steps:

1. The employment of a new executive who will succeed because his or her personality, skills, values, and experience align with the organisation's culture and strategic direction.

2. Effective handover which is generally shorter (less than two weeks) than longer.

3. The outgoing executive making a clean break with the organisation that brings closure and a sense of the value of the executive's tenure.

Lear failed on all three counts and became a lame-duck CEO.

Honey catches more flies than vinegar

Shakespeare himself dislikes flattery. He knows that flattery is generally shallow and self-serving:

> 'That sir which serves and seeks for gain,
> And follows but for form,
> Will pack, when it begins to rain,
> And leave thee to the storm.'

However, he is also realistic and knows that flattery is a most potent weapon particularly among the rich and powerful.

> 'Through tattered clothes small vices do appear; Robes and furred gowns hide all.'

The reality is that of all the components, the H and the P most desire power. Hs want power for the material benefits that it brings; Ps like power because in satisfies their key desire: the desire to win. And flattery is a tactic that works well with Ps and Hs. Goneril and Regan use flattery successfully with their father, and later try to use flattery to gain the favour of Edmund, much to his amusement.

Managers and employees who are subordinate to a manager will do well to remember that being blunt and truthful to a P or an H is not often the optimal strategy. In the play Kent, who has been a faithful adviser to Lear during his long reign, tries to get Lear to reverse his decision to abandon his daughter.

Lear warns Kent not to do so: *'Come not between the dragon and his wrath.'*

However Kent believes Lear is being foolish and unjust. He begins by making the telling point: *'Duty will have dread to speak when power to flattery bows.'*

He bluntly argues that Lear should reverse his decision to split the kingdom and leave Cordelia with nothing. However, his blunt advice is rejected and Lear banishes Kent from the kingdom. Unfortunately, and particularly with high Ps, it is very common for the messenger to be blamed for telling the truth and presenting an unwanted message.

The sky is full of unexpected thunderstorms

This is the first half of a Chinese proverb. The second half goes: 'Life is full of unexpected misfortunes.' What this means is that the world is not naturally a happy place. In fact it is the opposite, in that things will more likely go wrong.

In *King Lear*, Shakespeare adopts the same point of view: *'As flies to wanton boys, are we to the gods, they kill us for their sport.'*

Shakespeare also makes the telling point that while problems can occur, you should not think it is the end of the world: *'The worst is not so long as we can say This is the worst.'*

He also states that trying to improve things is not always the best strategy: *'Striving to better, oft we mar what's well.'*

These three quotes provide the basis of what to believe and how to act as a manager.

1. First, while it is important to plan, it is also important to remember that things generally do not go as intended.

2. However, when things do go wrong, do not exaggerate the problems that occur. A little reflection will often make you realise that things could be much worse.

3. Finally when you have suddenly come up with the brilliant idea, or your subordinates are pushing you to buy a new piece of capital equipment, sleep on it and try to think of the problems. Managers often believe that like the military they have only two options, to attack or to retreat. They forget the third alternative is often the best: which is to stand your ground and do nothing.

Lessons for Life

Treat your children well

A major problem for managers is that they sacrifice family for work. Lear is a good example of someone who probably did this. The time he spent carving out an empire was time he did not spend with Goneril and Reagan. He probably had more time to spend with Cordelia and so was able to connect emotionally with her. However, a key lesson of play is that how you treat your children when they are young and vulnerable and dependent on you, is exactly the way they will treat you when you are old and vulnerable and dependent on them. Lear compounds the problem by demanding an unreal and impossible love from each of them and becomes disillusioned by each of them in turn. As a high P he thinks he is never wrong and has unrealistic expectations of his children.

This theme of filial ingratitude also plays out in the subplot of Gloucester and Edmund. Edmund's high H component makes his jealousy of his legitimate brother even more pernicious. However, you should also remember that Edmund has been abroad since childhood and would have had no parental love. Even worse Gloucester intends to send Edmund overseas again.

One key lesson that parents can give their children is to develop their Normal. This is particular important for people that have a high Hustler component such as Goneril, Regan and Edmund. A key aspect of the Normal is self-control which is reflected in the ability of a person to wait for things they want. This trait is arguably critical for life success. Hustlers in particular seek instant gratification.

The marshmallow experiment is a famous test of this concept and is mentioned by Daniel Goleman in *Emotional Intelligence*. In the 1960s a group of four-year olds were tested by being given a marshmallow and promised another, if they could wait 20 minutes before eating the first one. Some children could wait and others could not. The experimenters then followed the progress of each child into adulthood, and demonstrated that those with the ability to wait were more successful in life than those who couldn't.

Children also teach their parents. As any parent knows your children are the only ones who will give you an honest appraisal. If self-awareness is the first step in developing emotional intelligence, the frank feedback of your children is probably the most useful path to follow.

Oh reason not the need

While in the beginning of the play Lear is a very high P with a declining N, deep down he does have sensitivity and during the play it gradually emerges. At the end of the play he realises and admits he has wronged Cordelia. The tragedy of Lear is that he learns what life is about, but it is too late. This applies to nearly all of us; our lives are full of mistakes. *King Lear* is a play about making horrible mistakes and then living to see just how horrible the results can be.

Lear first realises his mistake when Goneril and Regan join together and refuse to allow Lear to keep his knights. When they ask him why he needs the knights, Lear realises that they are rejecting him and replies: *'Oh reason not the need.'* Lear is telling them that he desperately needs the knights for emotional reasons and they, his children, must take this on trust. You just have to accept it, as trust is the basis of human life. If you start arguing with my emotional needs, then we will all end up stark naked, unable to trust each other over anything. Of course he is asking two Hustlers to do this and the fatal flaw of the H is that deep down they do not trust anyone.

At this moment Lear begins to develop self-understanding. Lear realises that his two elder daughters not only do not love or trust him, but worse, they despise him. Then he realises that he has banished the only daughter who actually loves him. Finally, and this is terrible for a P, he realises he is powerless to do anything because he has given his power away. In a rage against his daughters he goes into the storm, where he begins by saying that if his family hates him, then mankind must be a cruel species. As the storm builds, Lear then begins to realise that the life he has led earlier was not one of compassion and humanity.

How not to turn into King Lear

Of course with people living longer, more and more children are having to face the King Lear problem. The parent makes the decision to retreat from life by declaring they are elderly before their time. Typically the child is being driven mad by parents saying, 'I'm old. What I do isn't important. I leave the world to you youngsters and by the way you are making a right mess of things, unlike us.'

Typically the parent, particularly if he or she has a lot of H or P and the child a lot of D, will use complaints, unfair demands, and self-pity as a way of controlling the child instead of living one's own life. The negative mindset is generally passed off as the inevitable result of old age. The parent fails to recognise that attitude is more important than condition.

How do we stop ourselves turning into clones of King Lear?

The answer is simple; adopt the activities and attitude of the high N.

We are what we do. Ns have the goal of self-improvement. Thus one key activity is to remain a student and learn new crafts and languages. Once travel was only the activity of the rich, now nearly everyone engages in the activity. For example in Australia the older people who travel around the country are known as the Grey Nomads. By learning about where you are going and the language, you can get a whole new lease of life. Another good activity is to develop and maintain at least some artistic or aesthetic pursuit. Again this can range from learning about and attending opera to joining a walking club and enjoying nature. Finally many Ns take up golf which is the perfect game for the N. It relies on honesty, players by the handicap system can measure their improvement, and there is a whole set of rules.

With regard to attitude Ns live by the rule first defined by the Greeks: 'Everything in moderation.' In the chapter on self-development we noted that this rule is a dynamic prescription. As an individual not only should we have self-awareness but we should learn to temper our strong drives and strengthen our weak ones. In addition we try to adopt N norms of thinking: people should consider us as ethical, logical and analytical in our approach to problems, consistent, courteous, and conservative.

This approach to life may be summed up by one of the great lines of Shakespeare: 'Men must endure their going hither even as their coming hence: Ripeness is all.'

Shakespeare is saying that while death is painful, as is childbirth to the mother, the secret to life is that we have to learn to endure hardship and adversity. We may not be able to grin and bear it, but we become adults by learning to bear it in a mature, unemotional way.

Death of a Salesman

Death of a Salesman was first performed in 1949 and won for Arthur Miller, then only thirty-five years old, the coveted Pulitzer Prize and many other awards. It is widely regarded as one of the great American dramas. The play is about a father in conflict with his two sons whose love and respect he ardently desires. The play skilfully uses flashbacks to reveal the discords and deceptions in the family and Miller is able to make telling comments about business and the American way of life.

Plot Summary for Managers

Death of a Salesman opens with Willy Loman returning unexpectedly to his New York home during the night. Although Willy had been on his way to Boston, he reveals to his wife, Linda that he had made it only to Yonkers before he had decided to return home. We learn that Willy has recently had several automobile accidents. Willy and Linda begin arguing about one of their sons, Biff, who has recently returned to New York from the West after quitting yet another farm job out West. Willy cannot understand why such an impressive lad is so lost.

Upstairs, Biff and his brother, Happy, who are spending the night at their parents' house, wake up and reminisce about their childhood, recalling their first flings with prostitutes. Biff is frustrated at his lack of professional success, but says he finds office work too routine and confining. Happy has a steady job but is younger, cockier and chases women. Both men discuss their dissatisfactions with their lives and Biff suggests they go west and start a ranch. Happy is tempted but wants to equal his boss in salary and prestige. He attempts to persuade Biff to move back to New York and suggests that Biff visit a man he once worked for, Bill Oliver, and ask for a loan so that the two of them can start a sporting goods business.

Much of the action in the play occurs as flashbacks, with Willy responding to the past as if it were the present. In the first flashback Willy remembers buying a much younger Biff and Happy a punching bag after they had proudly and energetically shined the family car. Biff is playing with a football he has stolen from his school. Willy begins bragging about how well liked he is as a salesman. Bernard, a cousin of Biff and Happy, enters and urges Biff to come study his math. According to Bernard, Biff is in danger of failing the course, hence failing to graduate, which would prevent him from accepting an athletic scholarship. Willy scoffs at the conscientious Bernard, saying his sons will succeed because they are better liked.

Willy and Linda begin to discuss their financial problems, which have increased because the firm that has employed Willy for decades has taken him off salary and put him entirely on commission. Willy brags about his big sales but then quickly cuts his estimates when he learns how much they need for car payments and household repairs. Willy then guiltily remembers a Boston buyer with whom he had an affair. Back in the present, Charley enters and begins a card game with Willy, who remains nervous and irritable. In another flash back, Willy recalls his older brother, Ben, who became rich by going to Africa and discovered diamonds. Charley warns Willy that Biff is stealing lumber from building projects, but Willy dismisses this as initiative and sneers at Charley and Bernard as unable to hammer nails.

Linda reveals their financial difficulties to her sons, but when they criticise Willy's firm, Linda claims Biff and Happy are equally neglectful. Linda also reveals that Willy has been trying to commit suicide, that his frequent automobile accidents seem to have been intentional, and that she has found a rubber tube near their gas water heater. She suspects that Willy will use the tube to asphyxiate himself with gas.

When Biff tells Willy that he is going to visit his former employer, Bill Oliver, Willy encourages Biff to ask to borrow $15,000 and act as if he were already prosperous. The first act ends with Linda pleading with Willy to go to his boss Howard and ask for a position that would not require him to travel.

The following day over breakfast Linda assures Willy that Biff had left in a good mood, confident that Bill Oliver will respond to him favourably. She tells Willy that they need $200 to cover the insurance premium, the final mortgage payment and some repairs. She also says that their sons want to take Willy to dinner that night.

Willy talks to his boss, Howard, but can hardly get his attention. Howard's sole interest is a costly new tape recorder. Howard then disclaims a Christmas party pledge to find Willy a position in New York rather than on the road and remains unyielding as Willy offers to work for less and less money. Willy begins shouting, citing his early success, which exasperates Howard, probably because Willy exaggerates his earlier abilities. By the end of the conversation, Howard fires Willy.

At this point, more flashbacks occur. First Willy remembers Ben urging him to seek his fortune in Alaska. Linda is frightened of Ben and his ideas and insists that Willy is doing well enough already: Willy then recalls the day of Biff's big high school football game in Ebbets Field. Biff and Happy (as teenagers) enter. Biff is in his football sweater and Hap carries the rest of Biff's uniform. Even Bernard wants to carry Biff's shoulder guards, but Charley chides Willy for letting a football game mean so much.

Returning to the present, Willy enters his brother Charley's office. He speaks with Bernard who is carrying tennis rackets and luggage and is off to Washington to try a case before the Supreme Court. Bernard asks what actually happened to Biff after high school, when he failed math and refused to make the course up over the summer. Willy becomes defensive and loud. As he frequently has, Charley offers Willy a job, but Willy is too proud to accept. Although he is disgusted, Charley continues to lend Willy money.

The scene shifts to Frank's Chop House, a restaurant where Happy is waiting for Biff and his father. Happy attempts to pick up a woman he assumes is a prostitute. When Biff arrives, he reveals that he has failed with Bill Oliver, who kept him waiting all day and didn't even remember him. Although Biff attempts to have a frank conversation with Willy, both Happy and Willy refuse to listen, ignoring the truth in favour of a fantasy. Within this conversation, another crucial flashback occurs. When Biff had failed math, he had gone to Boston to persuade Willy to intervene with the teacher. Instead, he discovered Willy in a hotel with another woman. Biff is distraught and refuses to attend summer school, giving up his opportunity for an athletic scholarship and a college education.

Biff and Happy leave Willy in the restaurant in order to accompany the prostitutes Happy had met earlier. The next morning, Linda is furious, and asks them both to leave and stop tormenting their father. Willy has clearly become unstable and goes out into the garden, planting seeds by flashlight. He holds an imaginary conversation with the phantom of Ben; they discuss the merits of committing suicide and claiming the insurance.

Biff appears and tells Willy he wants to say good-bye because he has decided to leave and not return. Biff becomes furious and storms out as he realises that Willy believes he is acting out of spite. Willy decides to commit suicide. The last moments of the play occur after Willy's funeral, which has not been well-attended. Biff indicates that he will return to the West, while Happy will remain in business in New York. The play concludes with Linda at Willy's grave, uttering the ironic remark that because their house is finally paid for (with Willy's insurance money), they are now 'free'.

Psychographic Profiles

Willy Loman

Willy is the salesman around whom the play is constructed. He is sixty-three years old, desperate to achieve even a small measure of the success to which he has always aspired, and does not want to face the reality that he has misdirected his energies and talents chasing a dream that has never materialised. Willy is highly emotional, unstable, uncertain at times, highly contradictory. Willy is mercurial and keeps changing his mind. In the first scene he is convinced that *'Biff is a lazy bum,'* but then Willy remembers how proud he was of Biff's popularity in high school and says: *'There's one thing about Biff—he's not lazy.'*

During his flashbacks and fantasies we see Willy's idealisation of himself as loving father and husband, a more capable provider; cheerful, light-hearted, popular and self-assured. However he is an unrealistic dreamer. In short Willy is a high M with low H and N.

Ms are full of optimism, and Willy is no different; the present is never as bad as it seems and the future will always be even better. Like many Ms, Willy exaggerates his successes. However he is sometimes brought back to reality when he admits recent trips have not been so profitable, once Linda began listing the household expenses. Trying to keep his own spirits up, as well as Linda's, Willy insists: *'Oh, I'll knock 'em dead next week. I'll go to Hartford. I'm very well liked in Hartford. You know, the trouble is, Linda, people don't seem to take to me.'* Willy's optimism falters and he has a sudden mood swing typical of an M when he tells Linda that he fears people see him as fat, foolish, and too talkative.

Unfortunately Willy, like many Ms, sees the world through rose-coloured glasses. At the end of the play Willy realises that he has failed to live up to his unrealistic expectations. He believes that by committing suicide he will be able to leave his family a $20,000 life insurance pay-off. Willy's certainty about the payout is another example of his wishful thinking; insurance companies are unlikely to pay someone who has purposely attempted fraud.

However, Willy Loman does not walk alone. Many people identify with Willy Loman. In a 1979 interview with Harry Rafsky on the Canadian Broadcasting Company, Miller asserted that after seeing *Death of a Salesman*, the audience members

' . . . were weeping because the central matrix of this play is . . . what most people are up against in their lives . . . they were seeing themselves, not because Willy is a salesman, but the situation in which he stood and to which he was reacting, and which was reacting against him, was probably the central situation of contemporary civilisation. It is that we are struggling with forces that are far greater than we can handle, with no equipment to make anything mean anything.'

Charley

Charley is Willy's only male friend, and eventually he becomes Willy's sole financial support, 'loaning' him fifty dollars a week knowing all the while that his money will never be repaid. Charley is a successful businessman: he is an H with commercial realism, but also has the high integrity of the N. Charley is exasperated by Willy's inability to separate reality and fantasy. Charley tries in vain to dispel Willy's delusions and attempts to save him from financial ruin by offering him a job. Willy however refuses his offer and Charley exclaims: *'You been jealous of me all your life, you damned fool!'* However it is not jealously motivating Willy, it is the combination of his high M optimism, and the lack of any N or H to bring him out of his fantasy world.

Willy provides another example of his high M low N temperament when he conveys to Charley his disbelief that Howard Wagner has failed to display the gratitude that Willy feels he deserves and has fired him. Charley realistically replies:

'Willy, when are you gonna realise that them things don't mean anything? You named him Howard, but you can't sell that. The only thing you got in this world is what you can sell. And the funny thing is that you're a salesman, and you don't know that.'

Despite his continued arguments with Willy, and despite the feelings of frustration and exasperation Willy arouses in him, Charley cares about his friend and offers him compassion and support.

Linda

Linda is a loyal and sympathetic D. She more than loves Willy, she admires him, even though he is mercurial, has massive dreams, and is temperamental. In contrast to Willy's M which generates affairs while he is travelling, Linda is a faithful wife.

She is loyal to Willy throughout the play even though she realises Willy is never going to be big success and make a lot of money. Nevertheless, she still regards him as better than her sons, even though she knows Willy is planning to kill himself. In one of the most powerful and moving theatrical speeches ever written, Willy's wife says:

> 'He's a human being, and a terrible thing is happening to him. So attention must be paid. He's not to be allowed to fall into his grave like an old dog. Attention, attention must be finally paid to such a person.'

A good example of Linda's cautious D behaviour is when Willy and Ben are discussing moving the family to Alaska. Linda counsels caution insisting that Willy is doing well enough already and asks: *'Why must everybody conquer the world?'*

However, she is not mindless and overly docile. She manages the household finances; she deals with Willy's unpredictable moods; and she detects when Willy tries to conceal things from her (such as the money from Charley and the hidden rubber pipe). Within the Loman family, Linda is perhaps the most rational person, but because of her gentle personality and because women of her day were not encouraged to be assertive, Linda rarely expresses any anger toward Willy or her sons. Her kind nature is momentarily interrupted when she scolds Biff and admits that getting along with Willy can be difficult; nevertheless, her temporary frustration actually signals her wish, like many Ds, that their family be happy and unified.

Biff

Biff is Willy's eldest son. While he was a high school football idol, he has grown into a man who, in his mid-thirties, displays only a small measure of his youthful confidence, enthusiasm, and affection. Biff strongest component is the Artist; he beats to a different drum and comes across as someone who is troubled and frustrated, with a tendency to escape into dreams. When Biff discovers that Willy was having an affair; he feels betrayed. However instead of getting on with his life, Biff stubbornly maintains the rage. Biff, who keeps stealing things as an adult, blames his father for not giving him the proper guidance when he was caught stealing as a child. Biff also blames his father for instilling in him the belief that success depends on money.

Biff ultimately decides to try to show Willy that his dreams and fantasies are false, telling his father: *'You were never anything but a hard-working drummer who landed in the ash can like all the rest of them! . . . I'm nothing, Pop.'*

In the Requiem scene at the play's end, Biff illustrates that he has truly come to an understanding of his father's failure to achieve success, observing that Willy *'never knew who he was'* and that he *'had the wrong dreams.'*

In the restaurant Biff begins to develop self-understanding, the first level of emotional intelligence: *'. . . I realised what a ridiculous lie my whole life has been! We've been talking in a dream for fifteen years. I was a shipping clerk'*

When Biff discovers Willy's affair, Biff like a true A remains silent and holds a grudge for the next 17 years. Once the loyal son, who took pride in his father's self-confidence, Biff now feels disgusted at Willy's shallowness. The Artist in Biff means that he beats to a different drum. He is now unable to pursue a career with any true seriousness because he is convinced business people like his father are 'fakes'. Willy, like many Ms who, while friendly to everyone, are often insensitive to their emotional drives, represses this incident and becomes convinced that Biff is trying to spite him by not building a career.

Happy

Happy is a Hustler with low Normal. His name is interesting. His father Willy is a Mover, and one of the core aims of the M is for everyone to be happy. Hence the name for his second son is not surprising.

Happy shows classic H behaviour in the restaurant scene. He introduces himself by pretending to work for a champagne company. When Biff arrives moments later, Happy continues lying; he pretends that Biff attended West Point and is now the quarterback for the New York Giants professional football team. He then helps Biff lie to Willy about the meeting with Oliver. He knows he should be helping his father, but as soon as he sees a pretty girl he forgets him. Happy denies Willy is his father trying in part to impress the women he has picked up. All this lying is classic H behaviour.

Happy, like a true H will sacrifice the long-term for the short. He preys on the fiancées and girlfriends of his bosses and often resorts to taking bribes. He talks about changing his ways and getting married but like many Hustlers never practises what he preaches.

At the end of the play Happy learns nothing from his father's failure and collapse; instead he declares that he will try to justify his father's dream of becoming a number one man.

Lessons for Managers

How important is EQ?

The modern management mantra is that EQ, Emotional Intelligence, is what determines success. What differentiates the successful business person is people skills. Interestingly Miller argues the opposite in *Death of a Salesman*. It is not a winning smile and attractive manner that succeed. Biff tries these but fails; his poor grades deprive him of a scholarship, his thefts eventually draw him a jail term.

Many EQ proponents would argue like Willy that what is important is personal attractiveness and who likes you. *'The man who makes an appearance in the business world, the man who creates personal interest, is the man who gets ahead.'*

Willy sounds like a classic people-skills coach when he starts rattling off advice to Biff about how to act and what to wear when he asks Oliver for the loan. Willy warns Biff not to tell Oliver jokes or use a boyish word like 'Gee,' but also not to be too modest because: *It's not what you say, it's how you say it—because personality always wins the day.'*

During the play, it is gradually revealed that Biff and Happy have become less and less successful by following Willy's advice. The contrast is then made with Bernard, who is a classic hard working Engineer with limited people skills. At the beginning of the play, Willy describes Bernard as anaemic. Later on he is amazed to learn from Charley that not only is his son, Bernard, going to argue a case in the Supreme Court but that in Willy's conversation with Bernard, he omitted to mention the success. Charley's remark—that Bernard does not have to mention something because *'He's going to do it'*—is telling. Miller contrasts the success of Bernard and Charley built on hard work, perseverance and commercial reality with the lack of success of Willy and Biff, who are driven by the desire to be well liked and come across as all talk and no action.

Can people confront the emotional reality about themselves?

One of the great themes of *Death of a Salesman* is the inability of the various characters to face the reality of their own emotions. Biff, unlike his brother and father, is the only one who does. Biff tries very hard to stop lying. After going to Oliver's office and stealing the pen, Biff finally understands how his life has been a *'ridiculous lie.'* He realises that he had begun believing the exaggerations and falsehoods that he, Willy, and Happy have always been so quick to make up. However, when confessing to dishonesty might mean pushing his father toward suicide, then Biff feels split and agonised. Happy, like Willy, can see no other alternative but continuing to deceive oneself and others. Determined to remain 'happy,' though he too may be suffering, Happy attempts to avoid both the agony Biff undergoes and the loss of control Willy experiences.

Willy must listen as Biff attributes his own failures largely to Willy: *'I never got anywhere because you blew me so full of hot air I could never stand taking orders from anybody!'* Willy refuses to accept Biff's idea that both of them are just ordinary, forgettable people, Willy bursts out: *'I am Willy Loman, and you are Biff Loman!'*

However Biff is beginning to understand himself and persists: *'Pop, I'm nothing! I'm nothing, Pop. Can't you understand that? There's no spite in it any more. I'm just what I am, that's al . . . Will you let me go, for Christ's sake? Will you take that phoney dream and burn it before something happens?'* Holding on to Willy, Biff begins to sob and then goes upstairs.

Willy however still remains in his own emotional dreamworld. Biff surprises Willy with his expression of affection, and Willy's mood changes. Convinced that Biff does not actually spite him but likes him, Willy declares: *'That boy—that boy is going to be magnificent!'*

In the Requiem scene Charley describes Willy as a salesman, with a smile on his face and a shoeshine. Biff, however, disagrees with Charley: *'Charley, the man didn't know who he was.'* Furious that Biff would say such a thing, Happy pledges to: *'. . . show you and everybody else that Willy Loman did not die in vain. He had a good dream. It's the only dream you can have—to come out number-one man.'* While Happy decides to stay in New York and refuses to face the emotional reality about himself Biff plans to leave, telling Happy: *'I know who I am.'*

The failure to face the emotional reality about themselves is matched by the distortions of their own memories. Although many of their stories have some historical truth, that truth is so covered with their euphemistic interpretations that it is barely recognisable. The stories the family has told have become nearly indistinguishable from the real circumstances of their lives. Trying to separate reality from fantasy, Biff says: *'Facts about my life came back to me. Who was it, Pop? Who ever said I was a salesman with Oliver?'* But Willy refuses to acknowledge the substance of the question: *'Well, you were.'* Biff contradicts him, as determined to acknowledge the truth as Willy is to deny it: *'No, Dad, I was a shipping clerk.'* Willy still declines to accept this fact without the gloss of embellishment: *'You were practically a salesman.'*

Later, the conversation among the three men reveals that similar embellishments continue to characterise their lives. *'We never told the truth for ten minutes in this house!'* Biff proclaims. When Happy protests that they *'always told the truth,'* Biff cites a current family lie: *'You big blow, are you the assistant buyer? You're one of the two assistants to the assistant, aren't you?'* But Happy continues the family habit: *'Well, I'm practically . . .'*

A major theme of emotional intelligence is that people should be able to understand their own emotional basis. Towards the end of the play Biff is groping his way towards a mature self-appraisal. Despite all their brushes with reality both Willy and Happy never take the first steps.

The failure of Willy to understand himself is the tragedy of the play. Willy is a man of limited talents who set himself unreasonable objectives based on overly high expectations. Instead of relying on real talents; he relied on 'personality'. Willy's real love was carpentry and working with his hands. Instead he tried to be a salesman, a career to which he was emotionally unsuited.

References

Badaracco, J L Jr, *Defining Moments*, Harvard Business School Press, Boston, 1997

Badaracco, J L Jr, *Questions of Character*, Harvard Business School Press, Boston, 2006

Bennis, W, 'The Julius Caesar Syndrome', Leading Edge, September 2003

Braun, N.J., 'Understanding temperament makes for a better boss', Rydges Magazine, Rydges, Sydney, July, 1975.

Braun, N.J., 'Self-interest needed by successful executives', Rydges Magazine, Rydges, Sydney, August, 1975.

Braun, N.J., 'Perennial fault-finder often a work bottleneck', Rydges Magazine, Rydges, Sydney, September, 1975.

Braun, N.J., 'The art of supervising shy individuals', Rydges Magazine, Rydges, Sydney, October, 1975.

Braun, N.J., 'Beware the Paranoid employee', Rydges Magazine, Rydges, Sydney, November, 1975.

Braun, N.J., 'Outbursts of irritation from placid workers', Rydges Magazine, Rydges, Sydney, April, 1976.

Cattell, R.B., *The Scientific Analysis of Personality*, Penguin Books, Middlesex, 1968.

Chandler & Macleod Consultants Pty. Ltd., *Human Relations Manual*, Sydney, 1972.

Clemens, John K and Mayer, Douglas F., *The Classic Touch: Lessons in Leadership from Homer to Hemingway*. Dow Jones-Irwin, Homewood, 1987

Crowcroft, Andrew, *The psychotic: Understanding Madness*, Penguin Group, London, 1967.

Eysenck, H.J. & Wilson, G., *Know Your Own Personality*, Maurice Temple Smith, London, 1975.

French, A. L., *Shakespeare and the Critics*, Cambridge University Press, London, 1972.

Gettler, Leon, *Organisations Behaving Badly*, John Wiley & Sons, Brisbane, 2005

Goleman, Daniel, *Emotional intelligence*, Bantam, New York, 1995.

Goleman, Daniel, Boyatzis, Richard E., and McKee, Annie, *The New Leaders: Transforming the Art of Leadership into the Science of Results*, Little Brown, London, 2002.

Granville-Barker, Harley, *Prefaces to Shakespeare*, B. T. Batsford Ltd, London, 1963.

Humm, D.G., 'Personality and Adjustment', The Journal of Psychology, 1942, 13, New York, 109-34.

Humm, D.G.E and Wadsworth, G.W.Jr., 'The Humm-Wadsworth Temperament Scale', American Journal of Psychiatry, 1935, 1, New York, 163-200.

Kermode, Frank, ed. *King Lear: A Selection of Critical Essays*, The Macmillan Press Ltd, London, 1969.

Littman, Robert, *Monarch Notes: Julius Caesar*, Simon & Schuster, New York, 1964.

Miller, Arthur, *Death of a Salesman*, The Viking Press, New York, 1949.

Nourse, John Thellusson, *Monarch Notes: Death of a Salesman*, Simon & Schuster, New York, 1965.

Rosanoff, A.J. *Manual of Psychiatry*, (6th edn), Wiley, New York, 1938.

Schucking, Levin L., *The Meaning of Hamlet*, George Allen & Unwin Ltd, London, 1966.

Schuettinger, Robert, *Monarch Notes: King Lear*, Simon & Schuster, New York, 1966.

Shakespeare, William. *The Tragedy of King Lear*, The Challis Shakespeare, Sydney University Press, Sydney, 1982.

Shakespeare, William. *King Lear*, French's Acting Edition, Samuel French Limited, London Sydney, 1967.

Shakespeare, William, *Hamlet* The Challis Shakespeare, Sydney University Press, Sydney, 1984.

Shakespeare, William, *Julius Caesar* The Signet Classic Shakespeare, The New American Library, New York, 1963.

Smith, F, 'The personalities that cause damage', Australian Financial Review, 15 November 2005.

Sophocles, *The Theban Plays : King Oedipus; Oedipus at Colonus; Antigone*, Penguin Group, London, 1947.

Storr, Anthony, *Churchill's Black Dog*, William Collins Sons & Co, Glasgow, 1989

Storr, Anthony. *Feet of Clay*, HarperCollins, London, 1996

Weinberg, George and Rowe, Dianne, *Will Power! Using Shakespeare's Insights to Transform Your Life*, St Martin's Press, New York, 1996.